To DAD

The Riverside Preachers

For our
favorite And
Another of the
great Preachers —

Laureen,
Jason,
Dan,

@hristmas '78

The Riverside Preachers

Fosdick   McCracken   Campbell   Coffin

Paul H. Sherry, Editor

Published by The Pilgrim Press
in cooperation with
the Fosdick Centennial Committee of The Riverside Church in the
City of New York

Cover and book design by Bill Davenport Studio
Line illustrations by J. Richard Kirk

Library of Congress Catalog Card Number 78–11812
ISBN 0–8298–0360–2

The Pilgrim Press, 287 Park Avenue South, New York, New York 10010

In honor of the one-hundredth
anniversary of the birth of
Harry Emerson Fosdick, May 24, 1878

Contents

Introduction

Preaching is in again! No longer is it fashionable to view preaching as an insignificant and dying art form. Rather, there is a renewed awareness that preaching is an indispensable means of communicating the good news of the Christian gospel. No one has made this point better than the apostle Paul. "How are [people] to call upon him in whom they have not believed? And how are they to believe in him of whom they have never heard? And how are they to hear without a preacher?" Paul's words still stand. The Christian church is in need of preachers who, in the words of Harry Emerson Fosdick, view preaching as "an exciting adventure" and who, week in and week out, preach the gospel in a compelling way.

The Riverside Church has been blessed with four great preachers —Harry Emerson Fosdick, Robert J. McCracken, Ernest T. Campbell, and William Sloane Coffin Jr. Through the years their preaching has related the Christian gospel with power to the lives of individual people and the struggles of a society in search of its soul. In and through their sermons God has come near to us in our times of need; we have been driven to our knees in repentance for our sin; visions of a world closer to God's intention have danced before our eyes; and our despair has again and again been replaced by a renewed hope.

Introduction

This volume, issued in honor of the one-hundredth anniversary of the birthday of Dr. Fosdick, includes twenty sermons by Riverside's four preaching ministers. Each one demonstrates how pursuasive the gospel can be when preached with conviction, imagination, intelligence and craftsmanship. We can think of no better way to honor the person generally recognized as America's greatest liberal preacher of the twentieth century—Harry Emerson Fosdick.

The basis for sermon selection has been threefold. First, we have sought to choose sermons that continue to be as alive today as when they were first delivered. Dr. Fosdick prayed silently before each of his sermons, "O God, some one person here needs what I am going to say. Help me to reach him." It is our hope that the sermons selected will reach you. Second, to demonstrate the scope of Riverside's preaching, we have included sermons that address both intimate personal concerns and pressing social issues. A distinguishing feature of Riverside's preaching has been and continues to be its concern for both the individual and the larger society because of a firmly held conviction that to stress one at the expense of the other is to preach an incomplete gospel. Finally, a number of sermons that have had an impact on national and international affairs have been included, not only because of their historical significance but because each one still has something to say to us. Several of these are highly controversial and exemplify the prophetic quality of the Riverside pulpit. They remind us that often the preacher's task is to carry on a "lover's quarrel" with the world Christ came to save.

The volume is introduced with a sermon entitled "Public Proclamation" by Jitsuo Morikawa, interim preaching minister of The Riverside Church from October 1976 to October 1977. In that sermon, preached during the search for the present senior minister of Riverside, William Sloane Coffin Jr., Dr. Morikawa argues that the single most important qualification for Riverside's senior minister should be one's ability as a preacher. Dr. Morikawa's statement is a convincing argument for the centrality of preaching in the life of the Christian church.

The book closes on a note of celebration. On May 24, 1978, one hundred years to the day after the birth of Harry Emerson Fosdick, Roger Shinn, Reinhold Niebuhr Professor of Christian Ethics at Union Theological Seminary and a former student of Dr. Fosdick,

Introduction

spoke to the Riverside congregation about "Harry Emerson Fosdick, Religious Reformer." Dr. Shinn's statement reflects both the insight of a scholar and the warmth of a friend.

Many people have contributed to the publication of this anniversary volume, particularly C. Frederick Stoerker, chairman of the Fosdick Centennial Committee, without whom the book could not have been published. Jean Andralliski, Paul A. Byrne, Anne Cleaves, Eugene Laubach, Mary Emily Peck, Eddie Mott Smith, and Frances Unsell conducted valuable research. Mary L. Sherry and Mildred B. Stoerker were supportive in many ways.

Finally, all of us who have worked on this volume want to express our appreciation to the families of the preaching ministers and to the members and friends of The Riverside Church whose support has contributed significantly to the shaping of Riverside's preaching ministry.

—Paul H. Sherry

Editor's note: The editor does not have the prerogative to change the language patterns of the preachers. Were the sermons to be preached today, more inclusive language probably would have been used.

Public Proclamation

by Jitsuo Morikawa

Riverside Church is in the historic process of selecting their new senior minister and, in that crucial process, the qualification that takes preeminent place for consideration is one's ability as a preacher. It seems ironical that in a culture where preaching is not recognized as a significant function, certainly not a crucial function in comparison with diplomacy, finance, education or the medical arts, that a church, Riverside Church, should place preaching as the supreme necessity, even above one's capabilities as administrator, or pastor, or counsellor.

It is true, Riverside's history and reputation have been around great preaching and great preachers: Fosdick, McCracken and Campbell; and it is widely accepted that Fosdick was probably the greatest preacher of this century, a century that produced an array of pulpit giants, many of whom were here in New York City. But to follow a great tradition in preaching is not reason enough to place preaching at its place of high priority. Nor is it legitimate to seek a great preacher in order to attract a crowd, who will once again, under the spell of oratorical skills, fill the nave up to the triforium. I have nothing against great crowds and am not particularly impressed with empty pews, but popularity is hardly the chief mark of preaching.

Why do we place preaching as the preeminent qualification for the senior minister of Riverside? And what do we mean by preaching, and how different is it from other means of human discourse? Are we looking for a talented entertainer who will have a mass appeal; an erudite scholar who will speak to the academic community and the more thoughtful people of our city; a person of psychotherapeutic insight who will speak to the deep personal problems; a great story-teller whose sermons will be charmingly alive with illustrations? These are all legitimate elements within the difficult equation of preaching.

Why should preaching have a place of priority in the life of the church? Because preaching is God's chosen means of redeeming, transforming, and reshaping human history. "For after that in the wisdom of God the world by wisdom knew not God, it pleased God by the foolishness of preaching to save them that believe." The earliest record of our Lord's ministry is described: "Jesus came into Galilee, preaching the gospel of God," and our Lord's manifesto makes prominent the place of preaching:

The Spirit of the Lord is upon me, because he has anointed me to preach good news to the poor. He has sent me to proclaim release to the captives and recovering of sight to the blind, to set at liberty those who are oppressed, to proclaim the acceptable year of the Lord.

All the great prophets of the Old Testament were preachers of the word of God, even Moses who protested, "Oh, my Lord, I am not eloquent, . . . but I am slow of speech." What greater sermon was preached than Isaiah's:

Comfort, comfort my people, says your God. Speak tenderly to Jerusalem, and cry to her that her warfare is ended, that her iniquity is pardoned, . . . Every valley shall be lifted up, and every mountain and hill be made low; the uneven ground shall become level, and the rough places a plain. And the glory of the Lord shall be revealed, and all flesh shall see it together.

Who can forget the stern words of Amos the preacher of judgment: "They sell the righteous for silver, and the needy for a pair of shoes, but let justice roll down like waters, and righteousness like an ever-flowing stream." Jeremiah was appointed a preacher to the nation, and when he complained he could not speak, and was only a youth, he was told, " 'Whatever I command you, you shall speak. Be not afraid of them, for I am with you to deliver you,' says the Lord. Then the Lord put forth his hand and touched my mouth," is the way Jeremiah describes his call to preach. The greatest preacher of all time, the apostle Paul—the church's preeminent preacher—confessed: "For necessity is laid upon me. Woe to me if I do not preach the gospel."

Why is preaching the most indispensable function in human society? Because "Christ is all, and in all" the alpha and omega, the beginning and end, and this is the gospel, the good news, and the gospel and preaching are inseparable. God's action in Jesus Christ continues in the act of preaching, as a repeated sacramental act, as a historicizing act of God's redemptive action; the supreme means by which God's redeeming action continues in human history. If the Roman Catholic Church celebrates the Mass as the reenacting of Christ's saving deed, the Protestant Church sees in the sacrament of preaching a fresh disclosure of the saving presence of Jesus Christ. We should affirm both. God in Jesus Christ is disclosed in human history through the sacraments of preaching and the Lord's Supper. This does not preclude other ways, various ways, by which God is made manifest—the world of nature, the events of history, even the "still small voice."

Therefore hope of the world resides in preaching as handmaiden, inseparable from the gospel, as body to spirit and word to thought, fire to burning, and light to the sun. The folly of the world is to assume life without reference to God, and there cannot be any reference to God without the unique activity in human history called preaching. For "how are men to call upon him in whom they have not believed? And how are they to believe in him of whom they have never heard? And how are they to hear without a preacher?" Not because preachers are unique persons; they are not unique, exceptional, or superior; but because of their unique calling to speak forth the word of the Lord, to tell a unique story, the story of Jesus Christ. Their authority does not reside in their person, but in the truth they proclaim, their credentials reside in the One to whom they bear witness; and the power of their message resides in the kingdom to which they point with hope.

Therefore the test of great preachers is whether their preaching dramatizes and contemporizes, actualizes, the life and ministry of Jesus Christ, reenacts the redemptive activity of God in Christ, touches us with the power of the new creation, transforms us with the presence of the One who makes all things new, reenacts the cross and resurrection, and invades our history with the new history of Christ. Yes, Riverside needs a great preacher because world history and its future are shaped by the gospel and its preaching, by Jesus Christ and his continuing activity made real through preaching.

And the senior minister Riverside Church calls must be a preacher to the nation, for that is what preaching means—a public proclamation of a public deed that has public meaning and repercussion. C.H. Dodd in his famous book *The Apostolic Preaching and Its Development* distinguishes between preaching and teaching and states that much of current so-called preaching is actually teaching, or "ethical instruction" or "exposition of theological doctrine." "Preaching on the other hand," states Dodd, "is the public proclamation of Christianity to the non-Christian world." The verb "to proclaim" is rooted in a word meaning "a town crier, an auctioneer, a herald or anyone who lifts up his voice and claims public attention to some definite things he has to announce."

Jeremiah is an appropriate model for a preacher, who testifies: "Now the word of the Lord came to me saying, 'Before I formed you in the womb I knew you, and before you were born I consecrated you; I appointed you a prophet to the nation.' " So were Moses, and Amos and Hosea and Isaiah. They addressed themselves to the nation; reminded the people of their national origin, their history, their early beginnings, "the rock from which they were hewn, and the quarry from which they were digged," the Lord to whom they owed their all: "I am the Lord your God, who brought you out of the land of Egypt, out of the house of bondage. I bore you on eagles' wings and brought you to myself."

Every great preacher in history has addressed his nation: Augustine, the Roman Empire; Savonarola, Italy; Luther, Germany; Calvin, Geneva and Switzerland; John Knox, Scotland; Wesley, England; Jonathan Edwards, colonial America; Martin Luther King Jr., Black and white America. Abraham Lincoln, described by church historian Sidney Mead in *The Lively Experiment* as the spiritual center of American history, said in his Second Inaugural:

Public Proclamation

"Both [North and South] read the same Bible, and pray to the same God; and each invokes His aid against the other." Obviously "the prayers of both could not be answered—[and] that of neither has been answered fully." Why? Because in the movements of human history "the Almighty has his own purposes."

Great preaching is thus addressed to a whole nation; "that God governed the universe not only in space but also in time" in the words of Perry Miller; and "every event, as Emerson was to note . . . was held in its place by the weight of the universe." What would Amos or Isaiah or Jeremiah or Paul proclaim to our nation today? God delivered peoples out of the bondage of many lands, of tyranny and poverty and injustice, and forged a dissimilar people into "a new race of men," and "from this promiscuous breed" has emerged "the American, this new man" in the words of Crèvecoeur. Lincoln spoke to the nation. It was preaching in the grand tradition of the gospel. Preaching mandated of God must speak to the nation's soul, to repent, confess its sins, to change its ways, "to do justice, and to love kindness, and to walk humbly with your God."

August 7, 1977

Harry Emerson Fosdick

Founding Minister of The Riverside Church

1930–1946

The preacher's business is not merely to discuss repentance but to pursuade people to repent; not merely to debate the meaning and possibility of Christian faith, but to produce Christian faith in the lives of his listeners; not merely to talk about the available power of God to bring victory over trouble and temptation, but to send people out from their worship on Sunday with victory in their possession.

—Harry Emerson Fosdick
The Living of These Days

Finding God in Unlikely Places

DESPITE THE POPULAR familiarity of this hymn we just have sung—"Nearer, My God to Thee"—many of us do not live up to it.

> *Though like the wanderer,*
> *The sun gone down,*
> *Darkness be over me,*
> *My rest a stone . . .*

that is not a likely place to feel nearer to God.

> *So by my woes to be*
> *Nearer, my God, to thee . . .*

that is not easy. We naturally find God in life's lovely experiences. "Praise God, from whom all blessings flow"—that is where we find him—in our blessings—but when darkness and disaster come, we commonly cry, Where is God?

One Englishman recently said this: "I don't know what I believe, but I don't believe all this 'God is love' stuff. . . . I've been in two world wars, been unemployed eighteen months on end, seen the missus die of cancer, and now I'm waiting for the atom bombs to fall. All that stuff about Jesus is no help." Well, did *you* never feel like that?

This morning we study the kind of person who in such difficult situations does not lose God, but finds him. We shall be back on Riverside Drive in a moment, but we start far away from here, out in the wilderness of Sinai some thirty-two centuries ago, where Moses, facing a desperate situation, heard the Divine Voice say: "The place whereon thou standest is holy ground."

Into that wilderness Moses had fled, a refugee from Egypt. In anger he had killed an Egyptian taskmaster who was beating an Israelite and, compelled to flee, he had escaped into the desert, to lose himself in the badlands. Whether one thinks of the public evils of his time under Pharaoh's tyranny, or of the slavery of his people in Egypt, or of his own personal fall from being the son of Pharaoh's daughter to facing the niggardly life of the sheep range, he was in an unpromising place; and it was news to him when, amid the sagebrush and the sand, the arresting message came that *that* place was holy ground.

Far from being merely thirty-two centuries old, that scene is here in this congregation now. We find God in life's lovely things—yes! God *is* in life's lovely things. But soon or late all of us come to the place where, if we are to find God at all, we must find him in a wilderness. How we admire people who do that! When Helen Keller says about her blindness and deafness, "I thank God for my handicaps, for through them I have found myself, my work and my God," that is something! I have found the divine in the Ninth Symphony, or in sunsets,

> *When the sun supine*
> *Lay rocking on the ocean, like a god,*

but to find God where Helen Keller found him, or Moses—that calls for insight.

Today we *all* need that insight. Not only does life land each of us in unpromising situations, but our whole era is tragic, desperately tragic. How does one find God here? Yet some of the most momentous discoveries of God in history have been made in just such situations. A verse in the book of Exodus has fascinated me for years, but I have never dared preach on it. Here it is: "And Moses drew near unto the thick darkness where God was." What a place to find God!

Nevertheless, that kind of experience has made history. In 1754 George Washington, in his early twenties, was on a tough spot. He had been defeated at Fort Necessity; he was accused of taking hasty action before reenforcements came, in order to get all the glory for

19

himself; his officers were called "drunken debauchees"; his report on French plans was denounced as a crooked scheme to advance the interests of a private land company. It looked like the end of George Washington. But now, Douglas Freeman, his biographer, looking back, writes this: "Just when one is about to exclaim about some mistreatment, 'What an outrage!' one reflects and says instead, 'What a preparation!' " So, from Moses to Washington holy ground has been found in a wilderness—what a preparation!

Well, what went on inside Moses that made possible his discovery of holy ground in the wilderness?

First, he found something to be angry at. He had been brought up as the son of Pharaoh's daughter, living a soft life, a playboy it may be, at the royal court. But as maturity came on, he began to be angry. How he must have fought against it—this disturbing indignation against something intolerably wrong, the slavery of his people! The more he grew up, however, the angrier it made him, until one day, seeing a Hebrew slave beaten by an Egyptian taskmaster, he was so mad that he slew the taskmaster.

That was foolish. That did no good. But at least this is to be said for Moses: he was no longer a playboy; he was angry at something unbearably wrong.

That was the beginning of the real Moses. His anger needed harnessing, but it was basic to all that followed. Said Martin Luther, centuries afterwards, "When I am angry, I preach well and pray better." Said William Ellery Channing, the great New England Unitarian minister, "Ordinarily, I weigh one hundred and twenty pounds; when I'm mad I weigh a ton." Anger is not ordinarily presented as a Christian virtue, but remember our Lord, of whom our earliest Gospel says that when he saw a deed of mercy being held up by a ceremonial triviality, he "looked round about on them with anger"; and that when he saw little children being roughly shoved aside, "he was moved with indignation." Paul did write the thirteenth chapter of First Corinthians on love, but he said also: "Be ye angry, and sin not." That is to say, Control it, harness it for good, but still in the face of some evils you are not a Christian if you are not angry. Great character is not soft; at its very core is indignation at some things intolerably wrong.

So in his grim generation Moses began his discovery of holy

ground, and when he came down from Sinai he carried with him ethical convictions that have shaken the centuries: "Thou shalt not kill. Thou shalt not commit adultery. Thou shalt not steal. Thou shalt nòt bear false witness against thy neighbor. Thou shalt not covet." So! His indignation against evil got him somewhere.

Need I expand the application of this to ourselves? Look at our world! It is hard to find God here, we say. Well, we can start. We can see the evil here that ought to rouse our indignation. We can see the everlasting right here calling for our backing and support. We can at least quit our moral apathy, and wake up to the momentous issues of right and wrong in this Manhattanville neighborhood, this city, this nation. That's where Moses started when he found holy ground in the wilderness.

This start, however, led him to a second step. Moses in the wilderness confronted Moses. He had never had such a searching look at himself before. Outward wrongs were there, demanding that someone set them right; but, if Moses was to help, he had to tackle Moses.

We had better get this austere aspect of our theme into the picture, because the whole idea of seeing divine meanings in life is so commonly sentimentalized.

> *The poem hangs on the berry-bush*
> *When comes the poet's eye;*
> *The street begins to masquerade,*
> *When Shakespeare passes by.*

That's true. Life is just as rich as we have the capacity to see. That's true. But that lovely aspect of the truth is not the whole of it. To confront oneself in a wilderness, to be told that *there* is divine opportunity, is a soul-searching experience. Tackle yourself! said God to Moses.

Of course Moses at first backed off from that. Who was he to do anything about the Egyptian situation? "Meek as Moses" is a cliché now. Well, Moses was far from being meek in any soft sense, but he was humble. All great character is humble. William Carey, one of the supreme figures in Christian history, a major pioneer in opening India to the gospel, in his elder, reminiscent years said: "If God could use me, he can use anybody." Moses was like that, and when at last on Nebo's top he surveyed the Promised Land, and recalled the long years in the wilderness, I imagine he said: "If God could use me, he

21

can use anybody." So, of course, he shrank at first from God's formidable call. But not finally! He confronted himself until he dedicated himself. He found his vocation in that wilderness. With God's help he would be Moses!

How often scenes like that have been the turning points of history! Once a man named Wilfred Grenfell landed in Labrador, on a gala vacation cruise, visiting for fun a strange coast. Landing on that bleak, inhospitable shore, however, he wrote afterwards: "I attended 900 persons who never would have seen a doctor if I had not been there." That got him. He *had* to come back. He *had* to identify himself with Labrador. A divine voice had said to him in a wilderness: The place whereon thou standest—holy ground.

God is saying that to someone here today about some situation —personal, domestic, social, national. It is dreadful, we may be thinking. Yes, but if a situation is dreadful, then there is need. Tragedy is simply *need,* spelled with different letters; and so opportunity to help is there; you can do something for somebody, not despite the fact that it is Labrador, but because it is Labrador.

> *The poem hangs on the berry-bush,*
> *When comes the poet's eye.*

Yes, but the real miracle arrives when the poem does not hang on a berry bush, but is deep hidden in a wilderness, or in Labrador, or in some forbidding personal tragedy, and *then* "comes the poet's eye." So the great souls have found holy ground in unlikely places. They have found their vocation there.

We come to grips with our central theme, however, when we follow Moses' experience to a deeper level. In this encounter with right against wrong, in this self-dedication for his people's sake, he came face to face with God. Whatever may have been his idea of God, it is clear from the record that he had not in the least expected to meet his God in *that* place. What kind of situation was that in which to encounter God?

Many of us are precisely in that state of mind. We habitually talk of God in terms of love, beauty, goodness, so that when we face a situation, in our personal experience or in the world at large, where love, beauty, goodness are singularly absent, we lose all sense of God. Where is he? we say. Our modern liberalism has contributed to this

state of mind. Sings James Russell Lowell:
> *God is in all that liberates and lifts,*
> *In all that humbles, sweetens, and consoles.*

That is true. Wordsworth sings of God as
> *A presence, . . .*
> *Whose dwelling is the light of setting suns,*
> *And the round ocean and the living air,*
> *And the blue sky, and in the mind of man.*

That is true. But if the *only* God a man has is the God who thus is seen in the lovely things of life, its beauty and graciousness, the light of its setting sun, its liberating and consoling hours, then, when he finds himself in some tough, dismaying experience, in a desert, where beauty, goodness, and loveliness seem absent, where has his God gone? In days like these I need the God who encountered Moses in the wilderness, who challenged Grenfell in Labrador, the God who confronts men in unlikely places.

As a matter of historic fact, some of the most memorable encounters with God in history have been of that type. Moses in the desert; the Great Isaiah in Babylon with his exiled people; Job, out of his tragic calamity saying to God, "I have heard of thee by the hearing of the ear; but now mine eye seeth thee"—the Old Testament is full of such experiences. As for the New Testament, there is Calvary. My soul! Crucifixion is not lovely. Who, casually looking on, could have found God there? But countless millions since, with hushed and grateful hearts, have seen that Calvary was holy ground.

It is no accident, I tell you, that man thus finds in tragic situations some of his profoundest insights into the Divine. Soft occasions do not bring out the deepest in a man—never! Rather, in formidable hours when loyalty to the right means the risk of everything, perhaps life itself; in dismaying generations when right is on the scaffold and wrong is on the throne; in personal calamity when God is no mere frosting on life's cake but the soul's desperate necessity—then have come man's profoundest religious insights and assurances. Where did Jesus say, "Not my will, but thine, be done"? In Gethsemane. When did Luther write,
> *A mighty fortress is our God,*
> *A bulwark never failing?*

When he faced a hostile emperor at the risk of his life. When did Sir Thomas More say, "I die, the King's good servant—but God's first"? On the scaffold.

I do not know where this truth hits you, but for myself, now in my elder years, I bear my witness. My deepest faith in God springs not so much from my Galilees, where God clothed the lilies so that "Solomon in all his glory was not arrayed like one of these," but from times when "the rain descended, and the floods came, and the winds blew," and God was there so that the house fell not. You know the familiar argument that the world is such a mess, its evil so senseless and brutal that we cannot believe in God. Well, the world's evil is a great mystery. It raises questions none of us can answer. But over against the souls who, because of the wilderness, surrender faith in God, I give you the souls who found him in the wilderness. They are a great company.

Let us look at some of them.

Can you think of anything much worse than being a hopeless alcoholic? That's a wilderness for you! Well, here is my friend, Mrs. Marty Mann. She was there. Thirteen years ago she was in that hell. Listen to her story of what happened there: "In the depths of my suffering I came to believe. To believe that there was a Power greater than myself that could help me. To believe that because of that Power —God—there was hope and help for me." So in the wilderness she found God, and, like Moses, she is today leading others from the desert to the Promised Land. Of how many lives is it true that they never would have seen the stars if it had not been for the night.

Or can you think of any much tougher situation a nation could go through than Britain experienced in the last war? I have quoted one Englishman who lost God then. But Edward R. Murrow tells us: *In the autumn of 1940, when Britain stood alone, when the bombers came at dusk each evening and went away at dawn, I observed a sign on a church just off the East India Dock Road; it was crudely lettered and it read: "If your knees knock, kneel on them."*
Thank heaven, the power to find holy ground in a wilderness did not die out in England, and with it came what Edward Murrow calls, "steadiness, confidence, determination."

Or let me be autobiographical, as I trust some of you are being now. In my young manhood I had a critical nervous breakdown. It was the most terrifying wilderness I ever traveled through. I dreadfully wanted to commit suicide. But instead I made some of the most vital discoveries of my life. My little book, *The Meaning of Prayer,* never could have been written without that breakdown. I found God in a desert. Why is it that some of life's most revealing insights come to us not from life's loveliness but from life's difficulties? As a small boy said, "Why are all the vitamins in spinach and not in ice cream where they ought to be?" I don't know. You must ask God that. But vitamins are in spinach and God is in every wilderness.

> *Out of my stony griefs*
> *Bethel I'll raise;*
> *So by my woes to be*
> *Nearer, my God, to thee,*
> *. . . Nearer to thee!*

Indeed, consider not only personal situations, but our world situation now. We have just celebrated Thanksgiving Day. Think then of the calamitous era of the American Revolution, so terrific that many then could perceive nothing but chaos and tragedy. Yet, beneath the surface, see what was going on! The thirteen colonies had been for years at bitter odds—sometimes at swords' points with one another. Then, in 1774, at the first Continental Congress in Philadelphia, Patrick Henry made a speech in which he said this:

Throughout the continent, government is dissolved. Landmarks are dissolved! Where are now your boundaries? The distinctions between Virginians, Pennsylvanians, New Yorkers, New Englanders are no more. I am not a Virginian but an American.

See what was going on for those with eyes to perceive! A nation was being born. One of our contemporary historians, describing that scene, exclaims: "Forty-three delegates sat spellbound, hypnotized altogether. It was crazy, what they had just heard; they knew it was crazy. An American—in God's name what was that?"

But Patrick Henry was right. And he would be right again if he could be here with us, and beneath all our seething turmoil could see the emergence of new germinative ideas of world unity and world citizenship. This era too is holy ground.

Play your part in it—large or small—against the little-mindedness, the prejudices, the hatreds that divide individuals and neighborhoods, races and nations! When Rip van Winkle went to sleep, the sign over his favorite inn bore the portrait of George III; when he woke up, it bore the portrait of George Washington. He had slept through a momentous revolution. Don't do that now! This is holy ground, and God is here.

Now, a brief final word. When any man thus finds God in *un*-likely places, one may be fairly sure that he has first found God in likely places. Some beauty has touched his life, some love has blessed him, some goodness has made him aware of God. If you have that chance now to discover the Divine, don't miss it! It is not easy to find God in an unlikely place. Start now by finding him in a likely place.

Beauty, goodness, loveliness are here. Nobility of character, un-selfish sacrifice, moral courage and lives through which a divine light shines, like the sun through eastern windows, are here. And Christ is here, full of grace and truth, in whom we can see the light of the knowledge of the glory of God. Find God in these likely places that you may find him in the unlikely places too.

November 30, 1952

Shall the Fundamentalists Win?

This sermon was preached in First Presbyterian Church, New York City, May 21, 1922. Dr. Fosdick sought understanding by both liberals and conservatives, but he was bitterly attacked by the fundamentalists, led by William Jennings Bryan. The ensuing controversy made Fosdick a world figure. To an entire generation he pointed the way past a then conventional orthodoxy to a faith that the modern mind could accept with conviction and joy.

THIS MORNING WE are to think of the Fundamentalist controversy which threatens to divide the American churches, as though already they were not sufficiently split and riven. A scene, suggestive for our thought, is depicted in the fifth chapter of the book of the Acts, where the Jewish leaders hale before them Peter and other of the apostles because they have been preaching Jesus as the Messiah. Moreover, the Jewish leaders propose to slay them, when in opposition Gamaliel speaks: "Refrain from these men, and let them alone: for if this counsel or this work be of men, it will come to nought: but if it be of God, ye cannot overthrow it; lest haply ye be found even to fight against God."

One could easily let his imagination play over this scene and could wonder how history would have come out if Gamaliel's wise tolerance could have controlled the situation. For though the Jewish leaders seemed superficially to concur in Gamaliel's judgment, they nevertheless kept up their bitter antagonism and shut the Christians from the synagogue. We know now that they were mistaken. Christianity, starting within Judaism, was not an innovation to be dreaded; it was the finest flowering out that Judaism ever had. When the Master looked back across his heritage and said, "I am not come to destroy, but to fulfill," he perfectly described the situation. The Christian ideas of God, the Christian principles of life, the Christian hopes for the future, were all rooted in the Old Testament and grew up out of it, and the Master himself, who called the Jewish temple his Father's house, rejoiced in the glorious heritage of his people's prophets. Only he did believe in a living God. He did not think that God was dead, having finished his words and works with Malachi. Jesus had not simply a historic, but a contemporary God, speaking now, working now, leading his people now from partial into fuller truth. Jesus believed in the progressiveness of revelation, and these Jewish leaders did not understand that. Was this new gospel a real development which they might welcome, or was it an enemy to be cast out? And they called it an enemy and excluded it. One does wonder what might have happened had Gamaliel's wise tolerance been in control.

We, however, face today a situation too similar and too urgent and too much in need of Gamaliel's attitude to spend any time making guesses at supposititious history. Already all of us must have heard about the people who call themselves the Fundamentalists. Their apparent intention is to drive out of the evangelical churches men and women of liberal opinions. I speak of them the more freely because there are no two denominations more affected by them than the Baptist and the Presbyterian. We should not identify the Fundamentalists with the conservatives. All Fundamentalists are conservatives, but not all conservatives are Fundamentalists. The best conservatives can often give lessons to the liberals in true liberality of spirit, but the Fundamentalist program is essentially illiberal and intolerant. The Fundamentalists see, and they see truly, that in this last generation there have been strange new movements in Christian thought. A great mass of new knowledge has come into man's possession: new knowledge about the physical universe, its origin, its forces, its laws; new knowledge about human history and in particular about the ways in which the ancient peoples used to think in matters of religion and the methods by which they phrased and explained their spiritual experiences; and new knowledge, also, about other religions and the strangely similar ways in which men's faiths and religious practices have developed everywhere. Now, there are multitudes of reverent Christians who have been unable to keep this new knowledge in one compartment of their minds and the Christian faith in another. They have been sure that all truth comes from the one God and is his revelation. Not, therefore, from irreverence or caprice or destructive zeal, but for the sake of intellectual and spiritual integrity, that they might really love the Lord their God not only with all their heart and soul and strength, but with all their mind, they have been trying to see this new knowledge in terms of the Christian faith and to see the Christian faith in terms of this new knowledge. Doubtless they have made many mistakes. Doubtless there have been among them reckless radicals gifted with intellectual ingenuity but lacking spiritual depth. Yet the enterprise itself seems to them indispensable to the Christian church. The new knowledge and the old faith cannot be left antagonistic or even disparate, as though a man on Saturday could use one set of regulative ideas for his life and on Sunday could change gear to another altogether. We must be able to think our modern life clear through in Christian terms, and to do that we also must be able to think our Christian life clear through in modern terms.

There is nothing new about the situation. It has happened again and again in history, as, for example, when the stationary earth suddenly began to move, and the universe that had been centered in this planet was centered in the sun around which the planets whirled. Whenever such a situation has arisen, there has been only one way out: the new knowledge and the old faith had to be blended in a new combination. Now the people in this generation who are trying to do this are the liberals, and the Fundamentalists are out on a campaign to shut against them the doors of the Christian fellowship. Shall they be allowed to succeed?

It is interesting to note where the Fundamentalists are driving in their stakes to mark out the deadline of doctrine around the church, across which no one is to pass except on terms of agreement. They insist that we must all believe in the historicity of certain special miracles, preeminently the virgin birth of our Lord; that we must believe in a special theory of inspiration—that the original documents of the scripture, which of course we no longer possess, were inerrantly dictated to men a good deal as a man might dictate to a stenographer; that we must believe in a special theory of the atonement—that the blood of our Lord, shed in a substitutionary death, placates an alienated Deity and makes possible welcome for the returning sinner; and that we must believe in the second coming of our Lord upon the clouds of heaven to set up a millennium here, as the only way in which God can bring history to a worthy denouement. Such are some of the stakes which are being driven, to mark a deadline of doctrine around the church.

If a man is a genuine liberal, his primary protest is not against holding these opinions, although he may well protest against their being considered the fundamentals of Christianity. This is a free country and anybody has a right to hold these opinions, or any others, if he is sincerely convinced of them. The question is: has anybody a right to deny the Christian name to those who differ with him on such points and to shut against them the doors of the Christian fellowship? The Fundamentalists say that this must be done. In this country and on the foreign field they are trying to do it. They have actually endeavored to put on the statute books of a whole state binding laws against teaching modern biology. If they had their way, within the church, they would set up in Protestantism a doctrinal tribunal more rigid than the pope's. In such an hour, delicate and dangerous, when feelings are bound to run high, I plead this morning the cause of magnanimity and liberality and tolerance of spirit. I would, if I could reach their ears, say to the Fundamentalists about the liberals what Gamaliel said to the Jews, "Refrain from these men, and let them alone: for if this counsel or this work be of men, it will come to nought: but if it be of God ye cannot overthrow it; lest haply ye be found even to fight against God."

That we may be entirely candid and concrete and may not lose ourselves in any fog of generalities, let us this morning take two or three of these Fundamentalist items and see with reference to them what the situation is in the Christian churches. Too often we preachers have failed to talk frankly enough about the differences of opinion that exist among evangelical Christians, although everybody knows that they are there. Let us face this morning some of the differences of opinion with which somehow we must deal.

We may well begin with the vexed and mooted question of the virgin birth of our Lord. I know people in the Christian churches—ministers, missionaries, laymen, devoted lovers of the Lord and servants of the Gospel—who, alike as they are in their personal devotion to the Master, hold quite different points of view about a matter like the virgin birth. Here, for example, is one point of view: that the virgin birth is to be accepted as historical fact; it actually happened; there was no other way for a personality like the Master to come into this world except by a special biological miracle. That is one point of view, and many are the gracious and beautiful souls who hold it. But, side by side with them in the evangelical churches is a group of equally loyal and reverent people who would say that the virgin birth is not to be accepted as an historic fact. To believe in virgin birth as an explanation of great personality is one of the familiar ways in which the ancient world was accustomed to account for unusual superiority. Many people suppose that only once in history do we run across a record of supernatural birth. Upon the contrary, stories of miraculous generation are among the commonest traditions of antiquity. Especially is this true about the founders of great religions. According to the records of their faiths, Buddha and Zoroaster and Lao-Tzu and Mahāvīra were all supernaturally born. Moses, Confucius and Mohammed are the only great founders of religions in history to whom miraculous birth is not attributed. That is to say, when a personality arose so high that men adored him, the ancient world attributed his superiority to some special divine influence in his generation, and they commonly phrased their faith in terms of miraculous birth. So Pythagoras was called virgin born, and Plato, and Augustus Cæsar, and many more. Knowing this, there are within the evangelical churches large groups of people whose opinion about our Lord's coming would run as follows: those first disciples adored Jesus—as we do; when they thought about his coming they were sure that he came specially from God—as we are; this adoration and conviction they associated with God's special influence and intention in his birth—as we do; but they phrased it in terms of a biological miracle that our modern minds

31

cannot use. So far from thinking that they have given up anything vital in the New Testament's attitude toward Jesus, these Christians remember that the two men who contributed most to the church's thought of the divine meaning of the Christ were Paul and John, who never even distantly allude to the virgin birth.

Here in the Christian churches are these two groups of people, and the question that the Fundamentalists raise is this: shall one of them throw the other out? Has intolerance any contribution to make to this situation? Will it persuade anybody of anything? Is not the Christian church large enough to hold within her hospitable fellowship people who differ on points like this, and agree to differ until the fuller truth be manifested? The Fundamentalists say not. They say that the liberals must go. Well, if the Fundamentalists should succeed, then out of the Christian church would go some of the best Christian life and consecration of this generation—multitudes of men and women, devout and reverent Christians, who need the church and whom the church needs.

Consider another matter on which there is a sincere difference of opinion among evangelical Christians: the inspiration of the Bible. One point of view is that the original documents of the scripture were inerrantly dictated by God to men. Whether we deal with the story of creation or the list of the dukes of Edom or the narratives of Solomon's reign or the Sermon on the Mount or the thirteenth chapter of First Corinthians, they all came in the same way and they all came as no other book ever came. They were inerrantly dictated; everything there—scientific opinions, medical theories, historical judgments, as well as spiritual insight—is infallible. That is one idea of the Bible's inspiration. But side by side with those who hold it, lovers of the Book as much as they, are multitudes of people who never think about the Bible so. Indeed, that static and mechanical theory of inspiration seems to them a positive peril to the spiritual life. The Koran similarly has been regarded by Mohammedans as having been infallibly written in heaven before it came to earth. But the Koran enshrines the theological and ethical ideas of Arabia at the time when it was written. God an Oriental monarch, fatalistic submission to his will as man's chief duty, the use of force on unbelievers, polygamy, slavery—they are all in the Koran. When it was written, the Koran was ahead of the day but, petrified by an artificial idea of

inspiration, it has become a millstone about the neck of Mohamme-
danism. When one turns from the Koran to the Bible, he finds this
interesting situation. All of these ideas, which we dislike in the Koran,
are somewhere in the Bible. Conceptions from which we now send
missionaries to convert Mohammedans are to be found in the Bible.
There one can find God thought of as an Oriental monarch; there too
are patriarchal polygamy, and slave systems, and the use of force on
unbelievers. Only in the Bible these elements are not final; they are
always being superseded; revelation is progressive. The thought of
God moves out from Oriental kingship to compassionate fatherhood;
treatment of unbelievers moves out from the use of force to the
appeals of love; polygamy gives way to monogamy; slavery, never
explicitly condemned before the New Testament closes, is nevertheless being undermined by ideas that in the end, like dynamite, will
blast its foundations to pieces. Repeatedly one runs on verses like this:
"It was said to them of old time . . . but I say unto you"; "God, having
of old time spoken unto the fathers in the prophets by divers portions
and in divers manners, hath at the end of these days spoken unto us
in his Son"; "The times of ignorance therefore God overlooked; but
now he commandeth men that they should all everywhere repent";
and over the doorway of the New Testament into the Christian world
stand the words of Jesus: "When he, the Spirit of truth, is come, he
will guide you into all truth." That is to say, finality in the Koran is
behind; finality in the Bible is ahead. We have not reached it. We
cannot yet compass all of it. God is leading us out toward it. There
are multitudes of Christians, then, who think, and rejoice as they
think, of the Bible as the record of the progressive unfolding of the
character of God to his people from early primitive days until the
great unveiling in Christ; to them the Book is more inspired and more
inspiring than ever it was before. To go back to a mechanical and
static theory of inspiration would mean to them the loss of some of
the most vital elements in their spiritual experience and in their
appreciation of the Book.

Here in the Christian church today are these two groups, and the
question the Fundamentalists have raised is this: shall one of them
drive the other out? Do we think the cause of Jesus Christ will be
furthered by that? If he should walk through the ranks of this congregation this morning, can we imagine him claiming as his own those

33

who hold one idea of inspiration, and sending from him into outer darkness those who hold another? You cannot fit the Lord Christ into that Fundamentalist mold. The church would better judge his judgment. For in the Middle West the Fundamentalists have had their way in some communities, and a Christian minister tells us the consequence. He says that the educated people are looking for their religion outside the churches.

Consider another matter upon which there is a serious and sincere difference of opinion between evangelical Christians: the second coming of our Lord. The second coming was the early Christian phrasing of hope. No one in the ancient world had ever thought, as we do, of development, progress, gradual change, as God's way of working out his will in human life and institutions. They thought of human history as a series of ages succeeding one another with abrupt suddenness. The Greco-Roman world gave the names of metals to the ages—gold, silver, bronze, iron. The Hebrews had their ages too—the original Paradise in which man began, the cursed world in which man now lives, the blessed Messianic Kingdom some day suddenly to appear on the clouds of heaven. It was the Hebrew way of expressing hope for the victory of God and righteousness. When the Christians came they took over that phrasing of expectancy and the New Testament is aglow with it. The preaching of the apostles thrills with the glad announcement, "Christ is coming!"

In the evangelical churches today there are differing views of this matter. One view is that Christ is literally coming, externally on the clouds of heaven, to set up his kingdom here. I never heard that teaching in my youth at all. It has always had a new resurrection when desperate circumstances came and man's only hope seemed to lie in divine intervention. It is not strange, then, that during these chaotic, catastrophic years there has been a fresh rebirth of this old phrasing of expectancy. "Christ is coming!" seems to many Christians the central message of the gospel. In the strength of it some of them are doing great service for the world. But, unhappily, many so overemphasize it that they outdo anything the ancient Hebrews or the ancient Christians ever did. They sit still and do nothing and expect the world to grow worse and worse until he comes.

Side by side with these to whom the second coming is a literal expectation, another group exists in the evangelical churches. They,

34

too, say, "Christ is coming!" They say it with all their hearts; but they are not thinking of an external arrival on the clouds. They have assimilated as part of the divine revelation the exhilarating insight which these recent generations have given to us, that development is God's way of working out his will. They see that the most desirable elements in human life have come through the method of development. Man's music has developed from the rhythmic noise of beaten sticks until we have in melody and harmony possibilities once undreamed. Man's painting has developed from the crude outlines of the cavemen until in line and color we have achieved unforeseen results and possess latent beauties yet unfolded. Man's architecture has developed from the crude huts of primitive men until our cathedrals and business buildings reveal alike an incalculable advance and an unimaginable future. Development does seem to be the way in which God works. And these Christians, when they say that Christ is coming, mean that, slowly it may be, but surely, his will and principles will be worked out by God's grace in human life and institutions, until "he shall see of the travail of his soul, and shall be satisfied."

These two groups exist in the Christian churches, and the question raised by the Fundamentalists is: shall one of them drive the other out? Will that get us anywhere? Multitudes of young men and women at this season of the year are graduating from our schools of learning, thousands of them Christians who may make us older ones ashamed by the sincerity of their devotion to God's will on earth. They are not thinking in ancient terms that leave ideas of progress out. They cannot think in those terms. There could be no greater tragedy than that the Fundamentalists should shut the door of the Christian fellowship against such.

I do not believe for one moment that the Fundamentalists are going to succeed. Nobody's intolerance can contribute anything to the solution of the situation we have described. If, then, the Fundamentalists have no solution of the problem, where may we expect to find it? In two concluding comments let us consider our reply to that inquiry.

The first element that is necessary is a spirit of tolerance and Christian liberty. When will the world learn that intolerance solves no problems? This is not a lesson which the Fundamentalists alone need to learn; the liberals also need to learn it. Speaking, as I do, from the viewpoint of liberal opinions, let me say that if some young, fresh mind here this morning is holding new ideas, has fought his way through, it may be by intellectual and spiritual struggle, to novel positions, and is tempted to be intolerant about old opinions, offensively to condescend to those who hold them and to be harsh in judgment on them, he may well remember that people who held those old opinions have given the world some of the noblest character and the most rememberable service that it ever has been blessed with, and that we of the younger generation will prove our case best, not by controversial intolerance, but by producing, with our new opinions, something of the depth and strength, nobility and beauty of character that in other times were associated with other thoughts. It was a wise liberal, the most adventurous man of his day—Paul the apostle—who said, " 'Knowledge' puffs up, but love builds up."

Nevertheless, it is true that just now the Fundamentalists are giving us one of the worst exhibitions of bitter intolerance that the churches of this country have ever seen. As one watches them and listens to them, he remembers the remark of General Armstrong of Hampton Institute: "Cantankerousness is worse than heterodoxy." There are many opinions in the field of modern controversy concerning which I am not sure whether they are right or wrong, but there is one thing I am sure of: courtesy and kindliness and tolerance and humility and fairness are right. Opinions may be mistaken; love never is.

As I plead thus for an intellectually hospitable, tolerant, liberty-loving church, I am of course thinking primarily about this new generation. We have boys and girls growing up in our homes and schools, and because we love them we may well wonder about the church that will be waiting to receive them. Now the worst kind of church that can possibly be offered to the allegiance of the new generation is an intolerant church. Ministers often bewail the fact that young people turn from religion to science for the regulative ideas of their lives. But this is easily explicable. Science treats a young man's mind as though it were really important. A scientist says to a young man: "Here is the universe challenging our investigation. Here are the truths we have seen, so far. Come, study with us! See what we already have seen and then look further to see more, for science is an intellectual adventure for the truth." Can you imagine any man who is worth while, turning from that call to the church if the church seems to him

The Church Must Go Beyond Modernism

In the middle 1930s, Dr. Fosdick became increasingly concerned that the church was too easily accommodating itself to contemporary culture. This sermon placed Fosdick in the vanguard of Christian liberals who believe that the role of the Christian church is to challenge modern culture.

IF WE ARE successfully to maintain the thesis that the church must go beyond modernism, we must start by seeing that the church had to go as far as modernism. Fifty years ago, a boy seven years of age was crying himself to sleep at night in terror lest, dying, he should go to hell, and his solicitous mother, out of all patience with the fearful teachings which brought such apparitions to the mind, was trying in vain to comfort him. That boy is preaching to you today, and you may be sure that to him the achievements of Christian modernism in the last half century seem not only important but indispensable.

Fifty years ago the intellectual portion of Western civilization had turned one of the most significant mental corners in history and was looking out on a new view of the world. The church, however, was utterly unfitted for the appreciation of that view. Protestant Christianity had been officially formulated in prescientific days. The Augsburg Confession was a notable statement, but the men who drew it up, including Luther himself, did not even believe that the earth goes round the sun. The Westminster Confession, for the rigorous acceptance of which the Presbyterian rearguard still contends, was a memorable document, but it was written forty years before Newton published his work on the law of gravitation. Moreover, not only were the mental patterns of Protestant Christianity officially formulated in prescientific days but, as is always true of religion, those patterns were sacred to their believers and the changes forced by the new science seemed impious and sacrilegious.

Youths like myself, therefore, a half century ago faced an appalling lag between our generation's intellect on one side and its religion on the other, with religion asking us to believe incredible things. Behind his playfulness the author of *Through the Looking Glass* had this serious matter in mind when he represented the White Queen as saying to Alice, "I'm just one hundred and one, five months and a day." Said Alice, "I can't believe *that!*" Said the Queen pityingly, "Can't you? Try again: draw a long breath, and shut your eyes." So the church seemed to be speaking to us.

Modernism, therefore, came as a desperately needed way of thinking. It insisted that the deep and vital experiences of the Christian soul with itself, with its fellows, with its God, could be carried over into this new world and understood in the light of the new knowledge. We refused to live bifurcated lives—our intellect in the late nineteenth century and our religion in the early sixteenth. God, we said, is a living God who has never uttered his final word on any subject; why, therefore, should prescientific frameworks of thought be so sacred that forever through them man must seek the Eternal and the Eternal seek man? So we said, and, thanks to modernism, it became true of many an anxious and troubled soul in our time that, as Sam Walter Foss expressed it in "Two Gods":

> He saw the boundless scheme dilate,
> In star and blossom, sky and clod;
> And as the universe grew great,
> He dreamed for it a greater God.

The Church Must Go Beyond Modernism

The church thus had to go as far as modernism, but now the church must go beyond it. For even this brief rehearsal of its history reveals modernism's essential nature; it is primarily an adaptation, an adjustment, an accommodation of Christian faith to contemporary scientific thinking. It started by taking the intellectual culture of a particular period as its criterion, and then adjusted Christian teaching to that standard. Herein lies modernism's tendency toward shallowness and transiency; arising out of a temporary intellectual crisis, it took a special type of scientific thinking as standard and became an adaptation to, a harmonization with, the intellectual culture of a particular generation. That, however, is no adequate religion to represent the Eternal and claim the allegiance of the soul. Let it be a modernist who says that to you! Unless the church can go deeper and reach higher than that it will fail indeed.

In the first place, modernism has been excessively preoccupied with intellectualism. Its chosen problem has been somehow to adjust Christian faith to the modern intellect so that a man could be a Christian without throwing his reason away. Modernism's message to the church has been after this fashion: When, long ago, the new music came, far from clinging to old sackbuts and psalteries, you welcomed the full orchestra and such composers as Palestrina, Bach, Beethoven, to the glory of God; when the new art came you did not refuse it but welcomed Cimabue, Giotto, Raphael, and Michelangelo, to the enrichment of your faith; when the new architecture came, far from clinging to primitive catacombs or the old Romanesque, you greeted the Gothic with its expanded spaces and aspiring altitudes; so now, when the new science comes, take that in too, and, however painful the adaptations, adjust your faith to it and assimilate its truths into your Christian thinking.

Surely that has been a necessary appeal, but it centers attention on one problem only—intellectual adjustment to modern science. It approaches the vast field of man's experience and need headfirst, whereas the deepest experiences of man's soul, whether in religion or out of it, cannot be approached headfirst. List as you will the soul's deepest experiences and needs—friendship, the love that makes a home, the enjoyment of music, delight in nature, devotion to moral causes, the practice of the presence of God—it is obvious that whereas, if we are wise, we use our heads on them, nevertheless we do not approach them mainly headfirst, but heart first, conscience first, imagination first. A man is vastly greater than his logic, and the sweep and ambit of his spiritual experience and need are incalculably wider than his rational processes. So modernism, as such, covers only a segment of the spiritual field and does not nearly compass the range of religion's meaning.

Indeed, the critical need of overpassing modernism is evident in the fact that our personal spiritual problems do not lie there any more. When I was a student in the seminary, the classrooms where the atmosphere grew tense with excitement concerned the higher criticism of the Bible and the harmonization of science and religion. That, however, is no longer the case. The classrooms in the seminary where the atmosphere grows tense today concern Christian ethics and the towering question whether Christ has a moral challenge that can shake this contemporary culture to its foundations and save us from our deadly personal and social sins. So the world has moved far to a place where mere Christian harmonizers, absorbed with the intellectual attempt to adapt faith to science and accommodate Christ to prevalent culture, seem trivial and out of date. Our modern world, as a whole, cries out not so much for souls intellectually adjusted to it as for souls morally maladjusted to it, not most of all for accommodators and adjusters but for intellectual and ethical challengers.

When Paul wrote his first letter to the Corinthians, he said that he had become a Jew to the Jews that he might win the Jews, and he intimated that he had become a Greek to the Greeks that he might win the Greeks. "I have become," he said, "all things to all men, that I might by all means save some." That is a modernistic passage of adjustment and accommodation. But that is not all Paul said. Had it been all, Paul would have sunk from sight in an indistinguishable blend with the Greco-Roman culture of his day and we should never have heard of him. When he wrote the second time to the Corinthians he said something else: "Come out from among them, and be ye separate, saith the Lord, and touch not the unclean thing." Church of Christ, take that to yourself now! Stop this endeavor to harmonize yourself with modern culture and customs as though they were a standard and criterion. Rather, come out from among them. Only an independent standing-ground from which to challenge modern culture can save either it or you.

The Church Must Go Beyond Modernism

In the second place, not only has modernism been thus predominantly intellectualistic and therefore partial, but, strange to say, at the same time it has been dangerously sentimental. The reason for this is easy to explain. One of the predominant elements in the intellectual culture of the late nineteenth and early twentieth centuries, to which modernism adjusted itself, was illusory belief in inevitable progress. So many hopeful and promising things were afoot that two whole generations were fairly bewitched into thinking that every day in every way man was growing better and better. Scientific discovery, exploration and invention, the rising tide of economic welfare, the spread of democracy, the increase of humanitarianism, the doctrine of evolution itself, twisted to mean that automatically today has to be better than yesterday and tomorrow better than today—how many elements seduced us in those romantic days into thinking that all was right with the world!

In the intellectual culture to which modernistic Christianity adapted itself, such lush optimism was a powerful factor, and the consequences are everywhere present in the natural predispositions of our thought today. In the little village of Selborne, England, the visitor is shown some trees planted by a former minister near his dwelling, so that he might be spared the view of the village slaughterhouse. Those trees are suggestive and symbolic of the sentimental illusions we plant to hide from our eyes the ugly facts of life. Especially we modernistic Christians, dealing, as we were, with thoughts of a kindly God by evolution lifting everything and everybody up, were deeply tempted to live in a fool's paradise behind our lovely trees!

For example, modernistic Christianity largely eliminated from its faith the God of moral judgment. To be sure, in the old theology the God of moral judgment had been terribly presented so that little children did cry themselves to sleep at night for fear of him and of his hell. Modernism, however, not content with eliminating the excrescences of a harsh theology, became softer yet and created the general impression that there is nothing here to fear at all. One of the most characteristic religious movements of the nineteenth century heralded this summary of faith:

The Fatherhood of God.
The Brotherhood of Man.
The Leadership of Jesus.

43

Salvation by Character.
The Progress of Mankind—
onward and upward forever.

Well, if that is the whole creed, this is a lovely world with nothing here to dread at all.

But there *are* things here to dread. Ask the physicians. They will tell us that in a law-abiding world are stern conditions whose fulfillment or nonfulfillment involve bodily destiny. Ask the novelists and dramatists, and at their best they are not lying to us as they reveal the inexorable fatality with which character and conduct work out their implied consequence. Ask the economists. They will tell us there are things to dread that lead to an inevitable economic hell. Ask even the historians and they will talk at times like old preachers about the God of moral judgment, as James Anthony Froude did when he said, "One lesson, and only one, history may be said to repeat with distinctness: that the world is built somehow on moral foundations; that, in the long run, it is well with the good; in the long run, it is ill with the wicked."

Indeed, cannot we use our own eyes to see that there are things here to fear? For this is no longer the late nineteenth and early twentieth centuries. This is the epoch after the first world war shook the earth to its foundations, and the God of judgment has spoken. My soul, what a world, which the gentle modernism of my younger ministry, with its kindly sentiments and limitless optimism, does not fit at all! We must go beyond that. Because I know that I am speaking here to many minds powerfully affected by modernism, I say to you as to myself: Come out of these intellectual cubicles and sentimental retreats that we built by adapting Christian faith to an optimistic era. Underline this: *Sin is real.* Personal and social sin is as terribly real as our forefathers said it was, no matter how we change their way of saying so. And it leads men and nations to damnation as they said it did, no matter how we change their way of picturing it. For these are times, real times, of the kind out of which man's great exploits have commonly been won, in which, if a man is to have a real faith he must gain it from the very teeth of dismay; if he is to have real hope, it must shine, like a Rembrandt portrait, from the dark background of fearful apprehension; if he is to have real character, he must achieve it against the terrific downdrag of an antagonistic world; and if he is to have a real church, it must stand out from the world and challenge it, not be harmonized with it.

In the third place, modernism has even watered down and thinned out the central message and distinctive truth of religion, the reality of God. One does not mean by that, of course, that modernists are atheists. One does mean, however, that the intellectual culture of the late nineteenth and early twentieth centuries, to which modernism adjusted itself, was predominantly man-centered. Man was blowing on his hands and doing such things at such a rate as never had been done or dreamed on earth before. Man was pioneering new truth and building a new social order. You young people who were not here then can hardly imagine with what cheerful and confident trust we confided to man the saving of the world. So the temptation was to relegate God to an advisory capacity, as a kind of chairman of the board of sponsors of our highly successful human enterprise. A poet like Swinburne could even put the prevailing mood into candid words:

> *Thou art smitten, thou God, thou art smitten; thy death is*
> *upon thee, O Lord.*
> *And the love-song of earth as thou diest resounds through the*
> *wind of her wings—*
> *Glory to Man in the highest! for Man is the master of things.*

Look out on the world today and try, if you can, to repeat those words of Swinburne and still keep your face straight! At any rate, if ever I needed something deeper to go on than Swinburne's sentimental humanism, with man as the master of things, it is now—a philosophy, namely a profound philosophy about what is ultimately and eternally real in this universe. We modernists were so disgusted with the absurdities of the old supernaturalistic theology that we were commonly tempted to visit our distaste on theology as a whole and throw it away. But theology means thinking about the central problem of existence —what is ultimately and eternally real in this universe. And in the lurid light of days like these it becomes clearer, as an increasing number of atheists are honestly saying, that if the eternally real is merely material, if the cosmos is a physical fortuity and the earth an accident, if there is no profounder reason for mankind's being here than just that at one stage in the planet's cooling the heat happened to be right, and if we ourselves are "the disease of the agglutinated dust," then to stand on this temporary and accidental earth in the face of this vast cosmos and try lyrically to sing "Glory to Man in the highest! for Man is the master of things," is an absurd piece of sentimental tomfoolery. And because I have been and am a modernist, it is proper that I should confess that often the modernistic movement, adjusting itself to a man-centered culture, has encouraged this mood, watered down the thought of the Divine, and, may we be forgiven for this, left souls standing, like the ancient Athenians, before an altar to an unknown god!

On that point the church must go beyond modernism. We have been all things to all men long enough. We have adapted and adjusted and accommodated and conceded long enough. We have at times gotten so low down that we talked as though the highest compliment that could be paid Almighty God was that a few scientists believed in him. Yet all the time, by right, we had an independent standing-ground and a message of our own in which alone is there hope for humankind. The eternally real is the spiritual. The highest in us comes from the deepest in the universe. Goodness and truth and beauty are not accidents but revelations of creative reality. God is! On that point come out from among them and be ye separate! As the poet imagined Paul saying:

> *Whoso has felt the Spirit of the Highest*
> *cannot confound nor doubt him nor deny:*
> *yea with one voice, O world, tho' thou deniest,*
> *Stand thou on that side, for on this am I.*

Finally, modernism has too commonly lost its ethical standing-ground and its power of moral attack. It is a dangerous thing for a great religion to begin adjusting itself to the culture of a special generation. Harmonizing slips easily into compromising. To adjust Christian faith to the new astronomy, the new geology, the new biology, is absolutely indispensable. But suppose that this modernizing process, well started, goes on and Christianity adapts itself to contemporary nationalism, contemporary imperialism, contemporary capitalism, contemporary racialism—harmonizing itself, that is, with the prevailing social status quo and the common moral judgments of our time—what then has become of religion, so sunk and submerged in undifferentiated identity with this world?

This lamentable end of a modernizing process, starting with

indispensable adaptations and slipping into concession and compromise, is a familiar phenomenon in religious history. For the word "modernism" may not be exclusively identified with the adjustment of Christian faith and practice to the culture of a single era. Modernization is a recurrent habit in every living religion. Early Protestantism itself, emerging along with a new nationalism and a new capitalism, was in its day modernism, involving itself and us in entanglements and compliances with political and economic ideas in whose presence we still are tempted to be servile. Every era with powerful originative factors in it evokes from religion indispensable adaptation, followed by further concessive acquiescences, which in time must be superseded and outgrown. Early Christianity went out from an old Jewish setting into a new Greek culture and never would have survived if it had not assimilated into its faith the profound insights of Greek philosophy. So in the classic creeds, like that of Nicæa, we have a blending of the old faith with the new philosophy, and in that process John and Paul themselves had already played a part. But alas, early Christianity in its adjustment of its faith to Greek culture did not stop with adaptation to the insights of philosophy. At last it adapted itself to Constantine, to the licentious court, to war, to the lucrative enjoyment of imperial favors, to the use of bloody persecutions to coerce belief. One after another, it threw away the holiest things that had been entrusted to it by its Lord until, often hardly distinguishable from the culture it lived in, it nearly modernized itself into moral futility. Lift up that history, as if it were a mirror in which to see the peril of our American churches.

It is not in Germany alone that the church stands in danger of being enslaved by society. There the enslavement is outward, deliberate, explicit, organized. Here it is secret, quiet, pervasive, insidious. A powerful culture—social, economic, nationalistic, militaristic—impinging from every side upon the church, cries with persuasive voices, backed by all the sanctions and motives most urgent to the self-interest of man: Adjust yourself, adapt yourself, accommodate yourself!

When Great Britain was as mad about the Boer War as Italy is mad today about the Ethiopian War, and all the forces of propaganda had whipped up the frenzy of the people to a fever heat, John Morley one night in Manchester faced an indignant, antagonistic crowd, and pleaded with his countrymen against the war. This is part of what he said:

You may carry fire and sword into the midst of peace and industry: it will be wrong. A war of the strongest government in the world with untold wealth and inexhaustible reserves against this little republic will bring you no glory: it will be wrong. You may make thousands of women widows and thousands of children fatherless: it will be wrong. It may add a new province to your empire: it will still be wrong.

John Morley did not call himself a Christian. He called himself an agnostic. But he was far nearer standing where Christ intended his church to stand than the church has often been.

We modernists had better talk to ourselves like this. So had the fundamentalists—but that is not our affair. We have already largely won the battle we started out to win; we have adjusted the Christian faith to the best intelligence of our day and have won the strongest minds and the best abilities of the churches to our side. Fundamentalism is still with us, but mostly in the backwaters. The future of the churches, if we will have it so, is in the hands of modernism. Therefore let all modernists lift a new battle cry: We must go beyond modernism! And in that new enterprise the watchword will be not, Accommodate yourself to the prevailing culture! but, Stand out from it and challenge it! For we face this inescapable fact, which again and again in Christian history has called modernism to its senses: we cannot harmonize Christ himself with modern culture. What Christ does to modern culture is to challenge it.

October 3, 1935

The Unknown Soldier

This sermon was Dr. Fosdick's Armistice Day sermon in 1933. After recalling his support for the First World War, Fosdick renounces war and pledges that never again would he support or sanction another, a pledge he kept during World War II.

IT WAS AN interesting idea to deposit the body of an unrecognized soldier in the national memorial of the Great War, and yet, when one stops to think of it, how strange it is! Yesterday, in Rome, Paris, London, Washington, and how many capitals beside, the most stirring military pageantry, decked with flags and exultant with music, centered about the bodies of unknown soldiers. That is strange. So this is the outcome of Western civilization, which for nearly two thousand years has worshiped Christ, and in which democracy and science have had their widest opportunity—the whole nation pauses, its acclamations rise, its colorful pageantry centers, its patriotic oratory flourishes, around the unrecognizable body of a soldier blown to bits on the battlefield. That is strange.

It was the warlords themselves who picked him out as the symbol of war. So be it! As a symbol of war we accept him from their hands.

You may say that I, being a Christian minister, did not know him. I knew him well. From the north of Scotland, where they planted the sea with mines, to the trenches of France, I lived with him and his fellows—British, Australian, New Zealander, French, American. The places where he fought, from Ypres through the Somme battlefield to the southern trenches, I saw while he still was there. I lived with him in his dugouts in the trenches, and on destroyers searching for submarines off the shores of France. Short of actual battle, from training camp to hospital, from the fleet to no-man's-land, I, a Christian minister, saw the war. Moreover I, a Christian minister, participated in it. I, too, was persuaded that it was a war to end war. I, too, was a gullible fool and thought that modern war could somehow make the world safe for democracy. They sent men like me to explain to the army the high meanings of war and, by every argument we could command, to strengthen their morale. I wonder if I ever spoke to the Unknown Soldier.

One night, in a ruined barn behind the lines, I spoke at sunset to a company of hand-grenaders who were going out that night to raid the German trenches. They told me that on the average no more than half a company came back from such a raid, and I, a minister of Christ, tried to nerve them for their suicidal and murderous endeavor. I wonder if the Unknown Soldier was in that barn that night.

Once in a dugout, which in other days had been a French wine cellar, I bade Godspeed at two in the morning to a detail of men going out on patrol in no-man's-land. They were a fine company of American boys fresh from home. I recall that, huddled in the dark, underground chamber, they sang:

> Lead, kindly Light, amid th'encircling gloom,
> Lead thou me on;
> The night is dark, and I am far from home;
> Lead thou me on.

Then, with my admonitions in their ears, they went down from the second- to the first-line trenches and so out to no-man's-land. I wonder if the Unknown Soldier was in that dugout.

You here this morning may listen to the rest of this sermon or not, as you please. It makes much less difference to me than usual what you do or think. I have an account to settle in this pulpit today between my soul and the Unknown Soldier.

The Unknown Soldier

He is not so utterly unknown as we sometimes think. Of one thing we can be certain: he was sound of mind and body. We made sure of that. All primitive gods who demanded bloody sacrifices on their altars insisted that the animals should be of the best, without mar or hurt. Turn to the Old Testament and you will find it written there: "Whether male or female, he shall offer it without blemish before the Lord." The god of war still maintains the old demand. These men to be sacrificed upon his altars were sound and strong. Once there might have been guessing about that. Not now. Now we have medical science, which tests the prospective soldier's body. Now we have psychiatry, which tests his mind. We used them both to make sure that these sacrifices for the god of war were without blemish. Of all insane and suicidal procedures, can you imagine anything madder than this, that all the nations should pick out their best, use their scientific skill to make certain that they are the best, and then in one mighty holocaust offer ten million of them on the battlefields of one war?

I have an account to settle between my soul and the Unknown Soldier. I deceived him. I deceived myself first, unwittingly, and then I deceived him, assuring him that good consequence could come out of that. As a matter of hardheaded, biological fact, what good can come out of that? Mad civilization, you cannot sacrifice on bloody altars the best of your breed and expect anything to compensate for the loss.

Of another thing we may be fairly sure concerning the Unknown Soldier—that he was a conscript. He may have been a volunteer but on actuarial average he probably was a conscript. The long arm of the nation reached into his home, touched him on the shoulder, saying, You must go to France and fight. If someone asks why in this "land of the free" conscription was used, the answer is, of course, that it was necessary if we were to win the war. Certainly it was. And that reveals something terrific about modern war. We cannot get soldiers—not enough of them, not the right kind of them—without forcing them. When a nation goes to war now, the entire nation must go. That means that the youth of the nation must be compelled, coerced, conscripted to fight.

When you stand before the tomb of the Unknown Soldier on some occasion, let us say when the panoply of military glory decks it with music and color, are you thrilled? I am not—not any more. I see there the memorial of one of the saddest things in American history, from the continued repetition of which may God deliver us —the conscripted boy!

He was a son, the hope of the family, and the nation coerced him. He was, perchance, a lover and the deepest emotion of his life was not desire for military glory or hatred of another country or any other idiotic thing like that, but love of a girl and hope of a home. He was, maybe, a husband and a father, and already, by that slow and beautiful gradation which all fathers know, he had felt the deep ambitions of his heart being transferred from himself to his children. And the nation coerced him. I am not blaming him; he was conscripted. I am not blaming the nation; it never could have won the war without conscription. I am simply saying that *that* is modern war, not by accident but by necessity, and with every repetition it will be more and more the attribute of war.

Last time they coerced our sons. Next time, of course, they will coerce our daughters, and in any future war they will absolutely conscript all property. Some old-fashioned Americans, born out of the long tradition of liberty, have trouble with these new coercions used as shortcuts to get things done, but nothing else compares with this inevitable, universal, national conscription in time of war. Repeated once or twice more, it will end everything in this nation that remotely approaches liberty.

If I blame anybody about this matter, it is men like myself who ought to have known better. We went out to the army and explained to these valiant men what a resplendent future they were preparing for their children by their heroic sacrifice. O Unknown Soldier, however can I make that right with you? For sometimes I think I hear you asking me about it:

Where is this great, new era that the war was to create? Where is it? They blew out my eyes in the Argonne. Is it because of that that now from Arlington I strain them vainly to see the great gains of the war? If I could see the prosperity, plenty, and peace of my children for which this mangled body was laid down!

My friends, sometimes I do not want to believe in immortality. Sometimes I hope that the Unknown Soldier will never know.

Many of you here knew these men better, you may think, than

The Unknown Soldier

I knew them, and already you may be replacing my presentation of the case by another picture. Probably, you say, the Unknown Soldier enjoyed soldiering and had a thrilling time in France. The Great War, you say, was the most exciting episode of our time. Some of us found in it emotional release unknown before or since. We escaped from ourselves. We were carried out of ourselves. Multitudes were picked up from a dull routine, lifted out of the drudgery of common days with which they were infinitely bored, and plunged into an exciting adventure that they remember yet as the most thrilling episode of their careers.

Indeed, you say, how could martial music be so stirring and martial poetry so exultant if there were not at the heart of war a lyric glory? Even in the churches you sing,

> *Onward, Christian soldiers,*
> *Marching as to war.*

You, too, when you wish to express or arouse ardor and courage, use war's symbolism. The Unknown Soldier, sound in mind and body— yes! The Unknown Soldier a conscript—probably! But be fair and add that the Unknown Soldier had a thrilling time in France.

To be sure, he may have had. Listen to this from a wounded American after a battle. "We went over the parapet at five o'clock and I was not hit till nine. They were the greatest four hours of my life." Quite so! Only let me talk to you a moment about that. *That* was the first time he went over the parapet. Anything risky, dangerous, tried for the first time, well handled, and now escaped from, is thrilling to an excitable and courageous soul. What about the second time and the third time and the fourth? What about the dreadful times between, the long-drawn-out, monotonous, dreary, muddy barrenness of war, concerning which one who knew said "Nine-tenths of war is waiting"? The trouble with much familiar talk about the lyric glory of war is that it comes from people who never saw any soldiers except the American troops, fresh, resilient, who had time to go over the parapet about once. You ought to have seen the hardening-up camps of the armies which had been at the business since 1914. Did you ever see them? Did you look, as I have looked, into the faces of young men who had been over the top, wounded, hospitalized, hardened up— four times, five times, six times? Never talk to a man who has seen that about the lyric glory of war.

Where does all this talk about the glory of war come from, anyway?

> *Charge, Chester, charge! On, Stanley, on!"*
> *Were the last words of Marmion.*

That is Sir Walter Scott. Did he ever see war? Never.

> *And how can man die better*
> > *Than facing fearful odds,*
> *For the ashes of his fathers,*
> > *And the temples of his gods?*

That is Macaulay. Did he ever see war? He was never near one.

> *Storm'd at with shot and shell,*
> *Boldly they rode and well,*
> *Into the jaws of Death,*
> *Into the mouth of Hell*
> *Rode the six hundred.*

That is Tennyson. Did he ever see war? I should say not.

There is where the glory of war comes from. We have heard very little about it from the real soldiers of this last war. We have had from them the appalling opposite. They say what George Washington said: it is "a plague to mankind." The glory of war comes from poets, preachers, orators, the writers of martial music, statesmen preparing flowery proclamations for the people, who dress up war for other men to fight. They do not go to the trenches. They do not go over the top again and again and again.

Do you think that the Unknown Soldier would really believe in the lyric glory of war? I dare you; go down to Arlington National Cemetery and tell him that *now.*

Nevertheless, some may say that while war is a grim and murderous business with no glory in it in the end, and while the Unknown Soldier doubtless knew that well, we have the right in our imagination to make him the symbol of whatever was the most idealistic and courageous in the men who went out to fight. Of course we have. Now, let us do that! On the body of a French sergeant killed in battle was found a letter to his parents in which he said, "You know how I made the sacrifice of my life before leaving." So we think of our Unknown Soldier as an idealist, rising up in answer to a human call and making the sacrifice of his life before leaving. His country seemed to him like Christ himself, saying, "If any man will come after me, let him deny himself, and take up his cross daily, and follow me." Far from appealing to his worst, the war brought out the best—his loyalty, his courage, his venturesomeness, his care for the downtrodden, his capacity for self-sacrifice. The noblest qualities of his young manhood were aroused. He went out to France a flaming patriot, and in secret quoted Rupert Brooke to his own soul:

> *If I should die, think only this of me:*
> *That there's some corner of a foreign field*
> *That is for ever England.*

There, you say, is the Unknown Soldier.

Yes indeed, did you suppose I never had met him? I talked with him many a time. When the words that I would speak about war are a blistering fury on my lips and the encouragement I gave to war is a deep self-condemnation in my heart, it is of that I think. For I watched war lay its hands on these strongest, loveliest things in men and use the noblest attributes of the human spirit for what ungodly deeds! Is there anything more infernal than this, to take the best that is in man and use it to do what war does? This is the ultimate description of war—it is the prostitution of the noblest powers of the human soul to the most dastardly deeds, the most abysmal cruelties of which our human nature is capable. That *is* war.

Granted, then, that the Unknown Soldier should be to us a symbol of everything most idealistic in a valiant warrior, I beg of you, be realistic and follow through what war made the Unknown Soldier do with his idealism. Here is one eyewitness speaking:

Last night, at an officers' mess there was great laughter at the story of one of our men who had spent his last cartridge in defending an attack. "Hand me down your spade, Mike," he said; and as six Germans came one by one round the end of a traverse, he split each man's skull open with a deadly blow.

The war made the Unknown Soldier do *that* with his idealism.

"I can remember," says one infantry officer, "a pair of hands (nationality unknown) which protruded from the soaked ashen soil like the roots of a tree turned upside down; one hand seemed to be pointing at the sky with an accusing gesture. . . . Floating on the surface of the flooded trench was the mask of a human face which had detached itself from the skull." War harnessed the idealism of the Unknown Soldier to *that.*

Do I not have an account to settle between my soul and him? They sent men like me into the camps to awaken his idealism, to touch those secret, holy springs within him so that with devotion, fidelity, loyalty, and self-sacrifice he might go out to war. O war, I hate you most of all for this, that you do lay your hands on the noblest elements in human character, with which we might make a heaven on earth, and you use them to make a hell on earth instead. You take even our science, the fruit of our dedicated intelligence, by means of which we might build here the City of God, and, using it, you fill the earth instead with new ways of slaughtering men. You take our loyalty, our unselfishness, with which we might make the earth beautiful, and, using these, our finest qualities, you make death fall from the sky and burst up from the sea and hurtle from unseen ambuscades sixty miles away; you blast fathers in the trenches with gas while you are starving their children at home by blockades; and you so bedevil the world that fifteen years after the Armistice we cannot be sure who won the war, so sunk in the same disaster are victors and vanquished alike. If war were fought simply with evil things, like hate, it would be bad enough, but when one sees the deeds of war done with the loveliest faculties of the human spirit, he looks into the very pit of hell.

Suppose one thing more—that the Unknown Soldier was a Christian. Maybe he was not, but suppose he was, a Christian like Sergeant York, who at the beginning intended to take Jesus so seriously as to refuse to fight but afterward, otherwise persuaded, made a real soldier. For these Christians do make soldiers. Religion is a force. When religious faith supports war, when, as in the Crusades, the priests of Christ cry, "Deus Vult"—God wills it—and, confirming ordinary motives, the dynamic of Christian devotion is added, then an incalculable resource of confidence and power is released. No wonder the war department wanted the churches behind them!

Suppose, then, that the Unknown Soldier was a Christian. I wonder what he thinks about war now. Practically all modern books about war emphasize the newness of it—new weapons, new horrors, new extensiveness. At times, however, it seems to me that still the worst things about war are the ancient elements. In the Bible we read terrible passages where the Hebrews thought they had a command from Jehovah to slaughter the Amalekites, "both man and woman, infant and suckling, ox and sheep, camel and ass." Dreadful, we say

The Unknown Soldier

—an ancient and appalling idea! Ancient? Appalling? Upon the contrary, that is war, and always will be. A military order, issued in our generation by an American general in the Philippines and publicly acknowledged by his counsel afterwards in a military court, commanded his soldiers to burn and kill, to exterminate all capable of bearing arms, and to make the island of Samar a howling wilderness. Moreover, his counsel acknowledged that he had given instructions to kill everyone over the age of ten. Far from launching into a denunciation of that American general, I am much more tempted to state his case for him. Why not? Cannot boys and girls of eleven fire a gun? Why not kill everything over ten? That is war, past, present and future. All that our modern fashions have done is to make the necessity of slaughtering children not the comparatively simple and harmless matter of shooting some of them in Samar, one by one, but the wholesale destruction of children, starving them by millions, impoverishing them, spoiling the chances of unborn generations of them, as in the Great War.

My friends, I am not trying to make you sentimental about this. I want you to be hardhearted. We can have this monstrous thing or we can have Christ, but we cannot have both. O my country, stay out of war! Cooperate with the nations in every movement that has any hope for peace; enter the World Court, support the League of Nations, contend undiscourageably for disarmament, but set your face steadfastly and forever against being drawn into another war. O church of Christ, stay out of war! Withdraw from every alliance that maintains or encourages it. It was not a pacifist, it was Field-Marshal Earl Haig who said, "It is the business of the churches to make my business impossible." And O my soul, stay out of war!

At any rate, I will myself do the best I can to settle my account with the Unknown Soldier. I renounce war. I renounce war because of what it does to our own men. I have watched them come in gassed from the front-line trenches. I have seen the long, long hospital trains filled with their mutilated bodies. I have heard the cries of the crazed and the prayers of those who wanted to die and could not, and I remember the maimed and ruined men for whom the war is not yet over. I renounce war because of what it compels us to do to our enemies, bombing their mothers and villages, starving their children by blockades, laughing over our coffee cups about every damnable thing we have been able to do to them. I renounce war for its consequences, for the lies it lives on and propagates, for the undying hatreds it arouses, for the dictatorships it puts in the place of democracy, for the starvation that stalks after it. I renounce war and never again, directly or indirectly, will I sanction or support another! O Unknown Soldier, in penitent reparation I make you that pledge.

November 12, 1933

Recovering Our Angels

WE THINK THIS evening about the Sadducees; and the reason for selecting them as the subject of our Christmas Eve meditation you will see when we set in contrast two verses from the New Testament. The first is from Luke's story of Christmastime: "And suddenly there was with the angel a multitude of the heavenly host praising God," and the other is from the twenty-third chapter of the book of Acts: "The Sadducees say that there is no resurrection, neither angel, nor spirit."

That is to say, the Sadducees did not believe in angels; no, nor in anything that angels represent. They were the most worldly-wise men of their generation, believing in what their eyes could see and their hands handle, hardheaded skeptics with no confidence in the spiritual world. The Sadducees were people who never could have kept Christmas. What could they make of a hymn that says

> O rest beside the weary road,
> And hear the angels sing!

One suspects at once that there is a good deal of the Sadducee in most of us. So far as angels taken literally are concerned, we do not believe in them either. Our forefathers used to believe in them very literally. To the ancient world God himself often seemed far off, throned in the heavens, and when men thought of the divine ministries they thought of special messengers who came from God and did his bidding. If a man was sick and recovered, an angel had come to him; if he was tempted and gained a victory, an angel had helped him— so vivid were angels to our fathers. But it is not natural for us so to think. We sing about angels in the church at Christmastime, but who mentions them during the working week? They are not literally and practically real to us any more. As a man faces his own thoughts candidly, he begins to think that perhaps he is a Sadducee.

Only nobody would ever want to be a Sadducee after he once had been personally acquainted with them. They are the most unlovely people in the New Testament. They represented the official priesthood of the nation, and used their position for selfish purposes in a shameless way. When Greece was in the ascendancy, then the Sadducees truckled to the Greeks—they were Hellenists then. When Rome was ascendant, then the Sadducees truckled to the Romans—they were Latinists then. Always they were political compromisers, the Quislings and Lavals of their time, trading with every power that was in control, and standing in with the established order. "Beware," said Jesus, "Beware of the leaven of the . . . Sadducees."

If now you ask what was really the trouble with them, is there any truer answer than to say that they had no angels; no, not anything that by any stretch of the imagination could be called an angel—no sense of the reality and nearness of the spiritual world, no consciousness of divine guidance into ways of mercy and benevolence, no confidence in spiritual forces, no pity, no unselfishness. Their lives were vacant of all that. They had no angels.

Ah, someone says in protest, you are making poetry of the angels now! Exactly! That is what the angels are—the poetic representation of the deep realities of the religious life, and for the lack of them how barren and prosaic our spirits often are! In the scripture itself the angels body forth the familiar and beautiful experiences of the human soul with the divine. When Jesus was tempted in the wilderness, and it is written that angels ministered unto him, who does not know what that means: divine help in a spiritual trial? When Jesus rejoiced over a returning prodigal and said that "there is joy in the presence of the angels of God over one sinner that repenteth," who does not know what that means when someone whom he loves comes home again and his heart is filled with more than earthly joy? When the Master says of the children, "Their angels do always behold the face of my Father," who does not understand his meaning: that every child is represented in the heart of God, and that it is not the Father's will that one should perish? That is just what the angels are—the poetry of the religious life, bodying forth the nearness, reality, and availability of the spiritual world.

If you say that our fathers often took them very literally, I say, undoubtedly they did. But whether you try to do that or not, what I am sure of is this: the experience for which the angels always stood —the nearness and sustenance and helpfulness of the spiritual world —we need as much as ever our fathers needed it. Many a man who is a Sadducee would be happy this Christmastime if he could see again

> . . . *those angel faces smile*
> *Which I have loved long since,*
> *and lost awhile.*

Consider, therefore, some of those influences in our generation that tend to steal our angels from us and make us Sadducees. In the first place, some of our scientific ways of thinking tend to cause that. Suppose we are dealing with a marvelous fresco of Michelangelo, before which we stand in admiration. Then some scientist comes and tells us: This beauty which you admire is created by physical elements that we can analyze and measure. It's as simple as that. I can take all the physical elements that make this picture, says the chemist, and, reducing the whole fresco of Michelangelo, can hand it to you in chemical formula. When that attitude is extended over the whole of life, how it steals our angels from us!

But, my friends, the whole truth about life is not so simple as that. Sir Edward Burne-Jones, for example, said about one of Michelangelo's pictures: "There is a lump of greasy pigment on the end of Michelangelo's hog-bristle brush, and by the time it has been laid on the stucco there is something there that all men with eyes recognize as divine." So! Greasy pigment, hog-bristle brush, and stucco—what is it that can take such things and out of them make frescos of divine beauty? How can we reduce that creative thing, spirit, into the physical elements that it employs? How can we take our human life and, draining the spiritual glory off, reduce it to physical formulae? Creative spirit is the fundamental reality, and to see that, to be sure about that, to know that from everlasting to everlasting spiritual life alone is real, and to feel the nearness and helpfulness and availability of the spiritual world—that is to get our angels back again.

Well, this is Christmas Eve, the time of poetry, when in any sensitive man's heart things well up that cannot be said in prose. One can tell anything there is to tell about a little child in scientific prose if by the little child we mean the physical side only, but if some of us should try to tell this Christmastime all that we think and feel about some little children, you would have to excuse us from saying it in prose. It has to be said in poetry.

Mrs. Browning tries to tell her husband what her love has meant. She cannot do that in prose. She even talks about angels:

> *First time he kissed me, he but only*
> *   kissed*
> *The fingers of this hand wherewith I*
> *   write;*
> *And ever since, it grew more clean and*
> *   white,*
> *Slow to world-greetings, quick with its*
> *   "Oh, list,"*
> *When the angels speak.*

Put that in prose if you can. Here tonight may some of us get our angels back again!

Once more, there are some people who have their angels stolen from them and are made into Sadducees, not by skeptical thinking but by the pressure of the rough and often brutal facts of life. One of the most beautiful stages in the development of any character is that happy and fortunate time of youth before the ideals of life are tarnished by this sordid world. Wonderful the days of a sheltered youth before he has been cheated or betrayed or lied about, when his confidence in life's beauty is like a mirror with no mist upon it. But a man cannot stay long in that happy state. You need no preacher to tell you how soon this tough business of living steals our angels from us. Those Sadducees were hardheaded, worldly-wise men, no newborn kittens they—they had their eyes open! They knew the rough side of life. They knew it so well that something besides their heads had grown hard; their hearts had grown hard too.

During the last war a poem was published in a European paper that praised the four elements of the universe—earth, water, fire, and air—and this is what the poem did. It praised the earth because we can dig trenches in it. It praised the water because we can use submarines in it. It praised fire because it belches from the cannon's mouth. It praised air because from it we can drop bombs. Such a Sadducean spirit can be begotten by the bitterness and ruthlessness of war until all the angels have gone away and all the elements of earth's life are glorified as instruments of violence.

Well, who does not feel on Christmas Eve how lamentable a thing such a Sadducean spirit is? Where are those Sadducees of olden time, so worldly-wise and practical? They seemed the great successes of their generation. And yet, today, two thousand years after, we are keeping the birthday of another kind of person altogether. We have changed our calendar so that the humblest events in our life are dated from the year when first he came. And he was not a Sadducee. He had his angels. That heavenly host that sang of goodwill above the plains of Bethlehem are symbols of his real angels—friendliness, unselfish love, mercy that knew no boundaries of race or circumstance or sin, goodwill, forgiveness that melted men's hearts, and ideals and faiths that roused their aspirations. Nobody ever knew, as he did, the nearness and reality and availability of the spiritual world. He had his angels and we know well this evening that the reason we keep Christmas is just that, for nobody permanently matters in human history except the people who have angels.

Last of all, there are some people who become Sadducees not through skeptical thinking and not through life's rough and tumble but through the disillusionment of personal trouble.

In an old picture we all have seen, the child Jesus runs with outstretched arms from the carpenter's door to his mother's waiting embrace, and lo! the sun from behind casts at the feet of the running child the shadow of the cross. He is not the only child who goes from the sunshine of a happy babyhood, where angels sing, into tragedy. More people are made Sadducees by the disillusionment of trouble than by any other one thing.

Well, Christmas Day brings its message for all such, for he whose birthday we celebrate won, as nobody else ever did, that spiritual victory over trouble. It is indeed beautiful to hear the angels over Bethlehem, but as maturity comes on there is another scene that means even more to us. Long years after that first jubilation was hushed, a man left eight disciples at a garden gate and, going in, left three more underneath the trees, and then went on alone to cast himself in solitude before the face of God and fight the hardest battle of his life. There in Gethsemane he gave up the last hope of escaping the cross, and having prayed that the cup might pass he prepared his spirit to drink the whole of it, and it is written that there appeared unto him beneath the olive tree an angel from heaven, strengthening him, and he went out confident and calm and strong. He had kept his angels. They did not simply sing above his babyhood; they were his sustenance and strength in his maturity. He never knew the nearness and reality and sustenance of the spiritual life so well as when most he needed it.

Your own hearts, my friends, will tell you in what way you specially are tempted to be a Sadducee. Is it skeptical thinking? Is it the roughness of life's struggle? Is it the disillusionment of trouble? Whatever be the special form of the temptation, may Christmastime bring to us all the restoration of our angels!

December 24, 1942

Robert J. McCracken

Preaching Minister of The Riverside Church

1946–1967

I was bred on expository preaching. I started with a text and stuck to it. But here [The Riverside Church] I changed to topical preaching —plopping right into a situation and later linking it to the Bible. This is also called "life situation" preaching.

—Robert J. McCracken
The New York Times, June 5, 1967

It's the Human Touch That Counts

SOME TIME AGO, walking on Riverside Drive, I saw a truck pull up sharply and draw into the side of the road. The driver climbed out of his cabin and made for a small boy who was struggling with a tricycle at the curb. "You can't get it up, Sonny," he said, and with one movement of his arm and the pleasantest of smiles he put the machine on the sidewalk. On the way back to the truck, happening to glance in my direction, he good-humoredly shrugged his shoulders and yanked his thumb in the direction of the boy who was already on the tricycle and riding away. Though I was close to the lad I hadn't noticed him or his plight. I had been busy with my thoughts and, until I heard brakes being applied, oblivious to what was going on. My heart warmed to that truck driver. What he did was a little thing, and a simple thing, but it showed that he hadn't lost the human touch.

With the rush of life so fast and feverish we are apt to lose the human touch, to forget that, next to bread, kindness is the food all mortals hunger for. It is easy to develop an impersonal, unfeeling attitude to people. We grow so that we don't notice need or misery or injustice. Opportunities of showing little courtesies or performing simple kindnesses pass us by. We keep people at arm's length. We become so self-engrossed that we almost shrink from human contact.

It's the Human Touch That Counts

What we need to cultivate is the quality of sympathetic imagination and understanding that enables us to put ourselves in the place of other people, to visualize their life, to see with their eyes, to think as they think and feel as they feel. I heard recently of a president of an industrial concern who was reproving one of his junior executives. "Why didn't you use your imagination, man?" he demanded. The reply he received was, "Sir, I have no imagination, only technical knowledge." In all walks of life there are too many persons of whom that sort of thing is true. The human factor doesn't weigh with them as it ought. They think in figures, see every problem in terms of a mathematical equation, produce all sorts of elaborate statistics about it. They work by rule and routine, interpret regulations soullessly, carry official formality to excessive lengths, strangle humanity with red tape.

I wonder whether we appreciate how essential the human touch is to real religion. A church is a poor affair, no matter how beautiful its sanctuary, no matter how stately its services of worship, if its members lack the quality of sympathetic insight and understanding that carries them out from preoccupation with themselves and their own interests and needs until the pains and pleasures of others become theirs also. Religion is a poor affair if it has to do only with the individual and God, if it is never translated into social action, if it does not make us kinder, more patient, more helpful, more generous in our relations with our fellows. On the last Easter Monday of his life Dr. Samuel Johnson wrote to his friend Taylor: "In the meantime, let us be kind to one another." Kindness may not be "all the creed this old world needs," but it does need it desperately. It is the absence of simple kindness that is responsible for a great deal of our unhappiness and our stupidity. There is not as much sin in the world as many of us think; there is a woeful, widespread dearth of sympathy and understanding.

Jesus had the human touch. He had an instinctive feeling for people, not for humanity in the mass but for individuals. Ellery Sedgwick offers a shrewd comment regarding Phillips Brooks.

I remember his vast, benevolent bulk filling my study like Gulliver in Lilliput. In the pulpit [his] torrential eloquence was all that tradition says, but after talking with him I remember wondering whether he did not love everybody too dearly to care especially for anybody.

How sharp the eyes of youth are! What a judgment for a student to offer of the greatest preacher in America in his day! Nobody can have felt about Jesus that he loved everybody too dearly to care especially for anybody. His interest in people was personal. It was his quickness in understanding, his instinctive care for their necessities that commanded their affection. In Dr. Moffatt's translation of the Gospel According to Matthew, there is an arresting sentence. "On entering the house Jesus noticed that Peter's mother-in-law was down with fever." That's the human touch. He had a quick eye, an outgoing nature, an alert and sensitive sympathy. Facts did not have to be brought to his attention. He could take a situation in at a glance. He was concerned with the concerns of others. Nothing human was alien to him. He noticed the patched garments of children, the long lines of men out of work, a poor widow in the temple putting into the offertory box a contribution far beyond her means.

It is from Jesus we learn that the human touch is the hallmark of real religion. Think of the parable of the good Samaritan. What is religion worth, it says, if it can see need and pass it by; if it is insensitive to suffering; if it is so taken up with rank and ritual, with organizations and committees, that it has no time to turn aside for an act of mercy; if it fails to note what it does not want to think of? This is to play at religion. It is to tithe mint and anise and cummin and neglect what is vastly more important—interest in people, a feeling for them, the instinctive humanity that reaches out a helping hand to them, if it be only by the offer of a cup of cold water.

According to Jesus the last judgment itself turns on whether a man has the human touch or not. On the right hand of the Judge are men and women who realize where they are with a gasp of surprise. How has it come about? The Judge tells them: "I was a hungered, and ye gave me meat." The reply mystifies them. "Lord," asks one of them, "when saw we thee a hungered and fed thee?" They do not remember. Their little acts of kindness and of love had long since been forgotten, but Jesus insists that they are decisive. "Inasmuch as ye have done it unto one of the least of these my brethren, ye have done it unto me." With the men and women on the left hand it was the other way. They could remember their good record and were ready to point to it, but they had forgotten the decisive fact about themselves —they were instinctively hard. "Lord," they complain, "when saw we thee a hungered, or athirst, or a stranger, or naked, or sick, or in prison, and did not minister unto thee?" And the Judge replies, "Inasmuch as ye did it not to one of these least, ye did it not to me."

With the example of Christ so clear and his teaching so explicit it is strange that more attention has not been given to this matter. It is the human touch that counts. It is the little, unremembered acts of kindness and love that are the best portion of a good man's life. You can't be self-engrossed and be much of a Christian. I receive a good many letters asking me to state categorically what I believe. Do I subscribe to this? Do I preach that? Am I liberal or conservative or neoorthodox in my theology? One correspondent recently impressed me as so label-conscious, so positive that a man's theology was the first and last and only determinative thing about him, that I had an almost uncontrollable impulse not only to write him and ask whether there weren't deeper questions but *to send him a questionnaire* with such inquiries as these: "Have you a quick eye, an outgoing nature, a heart tender and sympathetic? Do you care when others are hurt? Are you swift to sense their hurt and to do what you can to relieve it? Is anything human alien to you?" We should have a quick eye, an outgoing nature, a heart tender and sympathetic. We should care when others are hurt—should be swift to sense and see their hurt and to do what we can to relieve it. Nothing human should be alien to us. This is the central and supreme simplicity of the religion of Jesus— to get alongside of people, to visualize their situation, to be understanding and sympathetic, to want to help and serve them. Yet that it is central and supreme can be tragically overlooked.

I have read of a minister doing his work in a hard, unimaginative fashion, neglecting none of his duties, sparing no pains in preparing his sermons. His visitation was ruled by a timetable which allowed only so many minutes to each household. If, through any accident, time was lost early in his round the later visits had to be curtailed in order that his full task for the day might be completed and he get home in time for dinner. One evening, entering the home of a very poor and very solitary woman, he looked at his watch and said, "I can only give you seven minutes." "Well," was the answer, "if that is all, you needn't sit down." He was thinking more of his carefully ordered plans and his punctual meals than of the woman in her chilling loneliness or of any trouble she might be in. He left her wounded and insulted, and she never forgot. It was lack of imagination, lack of the human touch, that poisoned everything.

Let me match that incident with another. For thirty-eight years W. H. Lax was a Methodist minister in the East End of London. He learned that an old man was gravely ill and called on him. It was at once made plain that he was an unwelcome visitor, for as soon as the sick man caught sight of Lax's clerical collar he turned his head and refused to utter a word. While trying to sustain a conversation Lax noted the dreariness of the room, the pitifully small fire, and suspected that provisions had run low. When he left he went to a butcher shop and had two lamb chops sent to the house. He called again a few days later and though the old man was still far from talkative he was disposed to be friendly. On the way home another order was left with the butcher. By the third visit there was a pronounced change in the patient. He was congenial and even expansive, and before taking leave of him Lax read from the scripture and prayed. A preaching engagement took him out of London for some days. When he got back he was informed that the old man had died and had left a message for him. Just at the last when he could barely speak he made a sign that he wanted to say something. "Tell Mr. Lax," he gasped, "it's all right . . . I'm going to God . . . but be sure to . . . tell him . . . that it wasn't . . . his preaching that changed me . . . it was . . . those lamb chops." How the human touch can break down barriers of misunderstanding and estrangement!

Mark how it does so. It is full of understanding—it knows how easy it is to sin, how difficult to live nobly. That is why it never makes quick, harsh judgments, never descends to personal abuse, is never sarcastic but seeks to win without wounding. It gets to the heart of a situation as nothing else can. It has an almost superhuman instinct for what ought to be done and how to do it. It is always rendering services that others never think of rendering or fail to recognize as requiring to be rendered. It prefers action to speech, and would rather visit someone in want than make orations about brotherhood. It believes in people and gives itself to them without reserve. It knows no barrier of rank or class, of creed or color. It never patronizes. It enters a slum with as much respect as a mansion. It thinks in terms of individuals—of men, women and children—and not in terms of "hands" or statistics.

It's the Human Touch That Counts

We need that spirit today. For the want of it our civilization is already in decline. In an age when space has been annihilated and the continents bridged, the world, shrunk as it now is, was never so full of strangers, nor the strangers so full of antagonisms. People seem to be without the quality of imagination and understanding, unable somehow to put themselves in the place of others, to visualize their life, to think as they think and feel as they feel. It's the human touch that is lacking.

We need it in the church. These are days when Christians have to demonstrate that belief in the love of God is more than a beautiful and sentimental idea. It cannot exist side by side with indifference to human need. It has to be translated into concern for people. It must find outward expression in action and in loving, self-denying service. Otherwise, turned in and made subjective, it is a subtle form of selfishness, an indulgence, a soporific, what Karl Marx complained all religion is—the opiate of the people, a ticket to heavenly happiness at a reduced price.

"Sentimentalism," George Meredith once said, "is enjoyment without obligation." Look at your religion in the light of that definition. At the end it will be what you have done for others, whether you had the human touch, that will count. Jesus' picture of the final judgment is breathtaking in its simple realism. It is not by our beliefs or our standing or our success but by our service and our love that we shall be judged. "Inasmuch as ye have done it unto one of the least of these my brethren, ye have done it unto me."

March 12, 1950

How to Deal with Loneliness

THE SERMON FOR today was suggested by an anonymous letter that a student sent to me. I do not think he would mind my sharing it with you. I believe he would be the first to agree that the problem with which he asks me to deal can best be grasped and dealt with if it is expressed in his own words.

This is what he wrote.

I wish you would devote one of your sermons to loneliness. I am a college freshman and am having a wretched time with the problem. All this emphasis here on learning to appreciate music and books and art seems false to me; they are no more lasting and ultimately satisfying than other diversions. What is the answer, then, to loneliness? I think it must be love, but it is so hard to be loved or to love. That is all I want to say.

Yours truly,

Perhaps I should indicate what my first reaction to the letter was. I wished that the writer had signed his name and supplied his address so that we could have met and talked together about his problem. Since that was impossible, I asked myself whether I should devote a whole sermon to the subject of loneliness. It would perhaps be helpful to a few, but what would it have to say to the majority? I was thinking of the student's problem as a peculiar problem. The more I thought, however, the more convinced I became that loneliness is not a peculiar problem, troubling a handful of folk and of no concern to people in general. At some time or other everybody has to reckon with it. It is one of the hardest tests a human being can face and it can be one of the most demoralizing of experiences.

If the student who wrote the letter is listening to me now I wonder whether his loneliness loses any of the sharpness of its sting from the reflection that the suffering it causes is not unique; it is not a doom spoken on him because of some failure or failing in himself; it is a sensation that is as common as breathing. There is a sense in which everyone is lonely. Each has his different road, his different trial, his different responsibility. We can live under the same roof with loved ones and not really know them or be known by them. There are invisible barriers between us so that even in fellowship we walk apart. I cannot express all that I am. No more can you. Gestures, speech, action are at best inadequate interpreters. The dullest has his dreams he never tells. The shallowest has his holy ground. There is an isolation of soul that is a great part of the pathos of human life. "In all the chief matters of life," says Amiel in his *Journal,* "we are alone; we dream alone; we suffer alone; we die alone."

It was a particular kind of loneliness though that was plaguing the student who wrote me. A freshman walking down Broadway can be as lonely as a traveler crossing a desert. There is no isolation of spirit like that experienced in great cities, no solitariness so desolating as when we are surrounded by droves of people who hurry past us too busy to see or to care. Nowhere are human bodies so jostled as in New York; nowhere perhaps are people so much alone. While director of the United Nations Medical Service, Dr. Frank Calderone testified to the difficulties Secretariat employees have in adjusting to life in this city. He stressed that the tall United Nations building in a sense "stratified" the jobholders into layers that impeded them from extending their friendships. "Many," he said, "become so lonely that they begin to exhibit such neurotic signs as worry and depression and physical symptoms like gastric ulcers and skin rashes." They came for help in such numbers that he soon realized he had an important problem on his hands. The service diagnosed case after case as loneliness, nothing more.

The young are not the only sufferers. With their haunting dreams and hidden conflicts and strong temptations they know all about sudden loneliness, but what of elderly folk? William James' saying, "The great source of terror to infancy is solitude," can be matched by Bronson Alcott's, "The surest sign of age is loneliness." Many today, living to a great age, are left alone, and they have to learn to be alone and yet not be lonely, a difficult achievement. When I preach about loneliness, I am not addressing a handful of folk and missing the mark in the case of the majority. The fight against loneliness begins early and stays late. Great numbers of people, young, middle-aged and old, are shut up like prisoners in the solitary confinement of their own tiny cells. They are afflicted by shyness or a sense of inferiority. They want, God knows, to be liked, need to be needed, hunger for friendship more than for bread, but they are unable to enter into other lives or to allow others to see into their lives.

How, then, does one deal with loneliness? The director of the United Nations Medical Service reports what he did with some fifty men and women complaining of a variety of minor ailments but whose root trouble was loneliness. He had a party thrown for them. Everybody had a wonderful time. Of the fifty not one had been back to the service since. For a woman, about to leave on a vacation, who had developed a neurotic pattern of behavior, the director really went out of his way. After learning that she was going to Cape Cod, he wired the Chamber of Commerce there and had her met by a brass band. He says she reported back to duty a changed woman. It is extraordinary what recognition, the human touch, a gesture of friendliness and friendship can do in building up the morale of tense and lonely souls.

At the same time, the director would almost certainly acknowledge that his measures would not prove a lasting or universal remedy. Throwing parties, going places, doing exciting things—these, scores of people have tried, only to find that the alleviation they afforded was temporary. Some lonely people make the mistake of spending their lives in running away from themselves. They take their holidays among crowds. They hurry on from one time-consuming experience to another. Louis Bromfield's novel, *Mr. Smith,* describes the type. Smith says:

I was tired, in the head and in the spirit. I think it came partly from never being alone, because in the world in which I lived nobody ever seemed to want to be alone. They seemed to have a terror of it. They all wanted to lunch together, or play golf together, or go to the country club or women's clubs together, or meet in the hotel bar or in the corner drugstore to kill time over the pinball machines. On their tombstone will be written, "He lived without ever being alive. Nothing ever happened to him."

That is not the way to deal with loneliness.

How should one deal with it? First, I would suggest this. *Draw out the resources within yourself.* Don't simply sit and brood. Be alert, ready to receive new impressions. Cultivate a mind broad and versatile, that has a wide variety of interests. Hold off any slackening or hardening of the arteries of body and mind for as long as you can. Keep your windows open, in every sense. Attempt at any rate to greet each new day on tiptoe. These are not the characteristics of mental youth; they are the characteristics of mental maturity. It is the mark of a mature person that, left to himself, he can people his solitude; he is able endlessly to interest, amuse and criticize himself.

So, smilingly, Katherine Mansfield said, "I really only have perfect fun with myself. Other people won't stop and look at the things I want to look at or, if they do, they stop to please me or to humor me or to keep the peace." So, smilingly, Thoreau said, "Why should I feel lonely? Is not our planet in the Milky Way?" So, proudly, J. M. Barrie said, "The greatest glory that has ever come to me was to be swallowed up in London, not knowing a soul, with no means of subsistence, and the fun of working till the stars went out. To have known anyone would have spoilt it. I did not even quite know the language. I rang for my boots, and they thought I said a glass of water, so I drank the water *and worked on.*" John Milton in his blindness might have been lonely but his work on his masterpieces, *Paradise Lost* and *Paradise Regained,* saved him from that. John Bunyan in Bedford Gaol might have been lonely, but read *The Pilgrim's Progress* and see how he peopled his solitude. These were persons always adding interests to their lives. Who was it that wrote—"If we are lonely, it is because we are blind or dumb or lazy!" A harsh saying? Yet we should not dismiss it without pondering over it. Draw out the resources within yourself.

The second suggestion I offer in dealing with loneliness is: *Get out of yourself and into the lives of others.* Avoid egocentrism as you would a plague, for it is a plague. Don't stand in your own light. Don't judge existence in terms of what it gives, and does not give, you. Don't reduce its range and scope to the cramping gauge of yourself. That is to look through the wrong end of the telescope. Turn it round. Look out instead of in. The cause of much loneliness is the failure to live for anything big enough or deep enough to satisfy the heart. There is that in all of us that will not be content with adding up figures, cooking and washing, running a business, buying and selling commodities. There must be something more in life or it will be flat, stale and unprofitable.

If you are ready to begin by giving and don't wait to be given, friends will not fail you—unless you demand of them a perfection you cannot offer in turn. You complain that you meet with no response, that you are passed by, that you are unpopular. Why is that? Are you by any chance wrapped up in yourself—cold, unobliging, indifferent to the welfare of others—and yet astonished that people do not like you? The self-centered life must be a lonely one. Shakespeare's twenty-ninth *Sonnet* supplies an illustration:

> *I all alone beweep my outcast state, . . .*
> *Wishing me like to one more rich in hope,*
> *Featur'd like him, like him with friends possess'd,*
> *Desiring this man's art, and that man's scope.*

Feeling so, what does one do? The answer is at the close of the *Sonnet:* "Haply I think on thee," and there and then Shakespeare is at "heaven's gate." Was "thee" a man or a woman? We do not know. What we do know is that it was someone outside his own circumscribed and wounded and sensitive soul, and in living for another he found himself.

So I say, Get out of yourself and into the lives of others. Be friendly if you would have friends. You know that you never forget the hand that was reached out to you in your hour of loneliness and despair. When you hear it said that being kind in that fashion is half the sum of all religion you at any rate are not inclined to dispute the statement. It is the people who live to themselves who are generally left to themselves. Somebody has said, "Until I loved, I was alone." So, speak a cheerful word to your neighbor. Offer a helping hand to those who are in difficulties. Sympathize when people are up against it and fighting a hard battle.

How to Deal with Loneliness

The world is wide, these things are small,
They may be nothing, but they are all.

The human heart is everywhere the same, and love is the key to it. Human beings are very much alike, whether Black or brown or white. In spite of differences, which they exaggerate, they have faiths, fears, hopes, needs and dreams in common—and love and loss and longing. If only we knew one another, trusted one another, helped one another, what a lovely world our world would be.

This is the ministry the church of Christ should be exercising. In John Henry Newman's phrase it should be "the home of the lonely." The dreadful anonymity of big cities should be unknown within its walls. There should be warmth in it and sympathy and friendship. They are sometimes lacking. I cite a case history from a young minister's notebook.

A great number of newcomers are simply chilled out of the church by the attitude of the old members. Here is a woman who, since the time of her marriage, twenty years before, has lost the habit of churchgoing. When she was a girl she lived in a country village, attended church with her family, took her first communion as a matter of social custom yet with complete sincerity. After her marriage she comes to live in the city, goes through the bitter, desperate years of the early thirties with a family growing up round about her, knows what poverty is. Her neighbors never go to church, have no time for it, regard it as something for the bosses. But one night she is called on by two girls from the parish church. She sees in them a picture of herself twenty years before. She wants to go back. Can we understand what it means for that woman to go to church again? It is not easy to make a decision like that. She comes to a service, happens to sit in the pew of a member who, God forgive us, asks her to move. Can we blame her for not coming back? Has she no heart to feel the insult? You can be certain that it will take more than a mission of visitation to bring her again into the so-called fellowship of Christ's people.

A quite exceptional case, you say. I wonder. Where churches are not "homes of the lonely" it may well be because their fellowship is not as real, as rich, as warm as it should be.

How to deal with loneliness? Draw out the resources within yourself. Get out of yourself and into the lives of others. Finally, *get closer to God.* Augustine is right. Our hearts will always be restless till they rest in Him. He is the only Reality, and we are real only insofar as we are in His order and he in us.

> *Our destiny, our being's heart and home,*
> *Is with Infinitude, and only there.*

Though you may not recognize that it is so, your heart and flesh cry out for the living God. Nothing less than God will ever finally meet your need. A soul adrift from God is a lonely, homesick soul. So many who have money, property, comfort, every material security, wonder why life has not yielded real happiness or abiding peace. It is because they are out of their native element, out of touch with the Source and Sustainer and Redeemer of their life.

Get closer to God. This was Jesus' secret. When foes turned on him, when friends forsook him, when the cross loomed up a ghastly reality, he said: "I am alone, yet not alone, for the Father is with me." Ah, friends, you and I build so largely on secondary securities which, when the big storms blow up, give and crash and let us down. It is Christ's faith in the fatherhood of God, in the nearness of God, in his love of us as individuals that draws out the resources within ourselves, gets us out of our own life and into the lives of others, and makes life to the last an adventure in friendship. Why, then, should the cry of the prodigal in his loneliness not be ours?—"I will arise and go to my Father."

October 24, 1954

The Marks of a Living Church

IN BRITAIN ONE SUMMER a prominent minister with whom I was discussing the state of religion in the country at large surprised me by saying, "The Church of England is dead, the Church of Scotland is dying." Looking back on the conversation I am sure that he did not mean me to take what he said literally. As I see it now, he was deliberately going out of his way to describe the current situation in arresting and alarming terms. He was anxious that I should appreciate how serious and critical it was. He knew, as we all do, that generalizations are to be avoided; they are as a rule too arbitrary; they are seldom comprehensive enough to cover all the facts. If he committed himself to a sweeping generalization it was because he wanted to bring home to me the plight and predicament of the British churches. He went on to speak at length about such matters as the decline in church attendance, the apathy of the rank and file of church members, the want of initiative and resource—even of competence—on the part of ministers, and the decreasing influence of the churches in national and international affairs. Many a time since we talked together, his deliberately provocative sentence has come back to mind: "The Church of England is dead, the Church of Scotland is dying."

It should be remembered that for men to talk so about the church is not new. In generation after generation there have been those who have dogmatically predicted its gradual decline and ultimate decease, though every time the deceased has proved too lively for the obsequies. When I was in the final year at the Divinity School in Glasgow, a minister came up from London to address the outgoing class. To this day I cannot make out why he was chosen to address us. He assured us that nationwide the trend was such that in ten years' time churches all over the country would be closing their doors, and in his case there could be no doubt that he meant literally every word he said. His bearing and demeanor indicated as much; he had the look of a beaten man. He was a false prophet. Not ten but twenty years have passed since he made his gloomy predictions, and while in many quarters church life in Britain may be in the doldrums, the churches are not closing their doors, or if by reason of the shifting population they are closed in one area they are soon opened in another. The church is an institution that never goes out of business. Subjected through the centuries to calumny, opposition, persecution; never an infallible institution; its representatives not what they ought to be; the assaults upon it from within sometimes greater, certainly more insidious, than those from without; its survival is one of the wonders of the world. Its continued existence and persistence for sixty generations is sheer miracle. "Sire," said Theodore Beza to King Henry of Navarre, "it belongs in truth to the church of God, in the name of which I speak, to receive blows and never to give them, but it will please your Majesty to remember that the church is an anvil that has worn out many a hammer."

That is a sentiment to match with the one I heard expressed in Britain. We do well to give good heed to both. We work on an enduring institution. There is no likelihood of its disappearance or decease. But anyone who knows, even in outline, the story of the church is aware that its course has been a checkered one and that if it has had periods of strength, it has not been unfamiliar with periods of weakness. There have been times, stirring times, when it has been a potent, pervasive, dynamic influence; when, as Jesus predicted would be the case, it has served like salt and light and leaven—making character, shaping thought, controlling events, influencing for good the designs and destinies of nations. There have been other times when its power has palpably dwindled and its influence shrunk, when it has been well-nigh moribund, affording neither light nor leading, with no prophetic voices to stir and challenge its own or the public conscience, without vitality or vision or gifts of leadership, having a name to live, yet at the point of death.

In the periods of its strength, its peak periods, what have been the marks of the church, its outstanding features, the qualities in its life and in its members that have caught the eye and held as well as attracted attention? Henry Ward Beecher commenced his ministry, as most preachers do, in a mood of optimism and elation. He expected to elicit a ready response from his hearers and to see interest in the work of the church growing and deepening. His hopes did not materialize; months passed and there was no perceptible stirring anywhere in the congregation; everything went on in ordinary, commonplace, uneventful fashion. He was at his wit's end and plagued with depression when one day the thought seized him: "There was a reason why, when the apostles preached they succeeded, and I will find it out if it is to be found out." From that moment he was on the right track. It is the same sort of strategy I have in mind when I suggest that it should be a rewarding exercise for us to look at the church in the periods of its strength and note what were then its most striking characteristics.

Take, for instance, *the sense of conviction.* That has all along been one of the marks of a living church. Whether in the first century or the sixteenth or the twentieth it has owed its vitality to the fact that its members have had a personal experience of Jesus Christ and have found in him and in his gospel a new interest in life, a master motive, a center for thought, an incentive to action. If they have been clear when others have been confused, absorbed when others have been distracted, confident when others in bewilderment have vacillated from one goal to another and from one interest to another, it is because they have discovered a star to steer by, a cause, a creed, a passionate attachment. No matter to what source you turn, and the sources are as varied as they are numerous—the letters of Paul, the *Confessions* of Augustine, the sermons of Luther, the hymns of Wesley, the theology of Schleiermacher, the biography of Elizabeth Fry, the autobiography of Grenfell of Labrador—you encounter people about whom the last thing to say is that they are dealing with propositions in the air or relying on rumor and hearsay. On the contrary, they are building on the proved facts of their own experience. They are speaking at firsthand. They have deep and thoroughgoing convictions, convictions that have spurred them to action, involved them in repeated self-sacrifice, and made ardent propagandists of every one of them. Suppose in this regard we do what Beecher did and go back for a criterion to the apostles. "I know whom I have believed," says Paul, and for him that is the fundamental matter from which everything stems. "It is no cunningly devised fables we are giving you," says Peter, "for we were eyewitnesses of Christ's majesty," and you can sense that having said that the man feels that for him there is no more direct, no more immediate court of appeal to which to turn. In the case of the apostle John, the stress is the same: "It is of what we have heard, of what we have seen with our eyes, of what we watched reverently and touched with our hands—it is about the Word who is the life that we are now writing." Who can fail to detect the note of conviction in those words, the glowing certainty, the intoxicating enthusiasm?

Those are qualities of which the church stands in urgent need today. The contention of Berdyaev, the Russian theologian, is incontrovertible:

There is no longer any room in the world for a merely external form of Christianity, based upon custom. The world is entering upon a period of catastrophe and crisis, when we are being forced to take sides, and in which a higher and more intense kind of spiritual life will be demanded of Christians.

Yet the dearth of robust conviction in the church is unmistakable. Where the fundamentals of the Christian religion are concerned there is among its members an alarming amount of vague and woolly thinking. To great numbers of them it has come to mean hardly anything more than being kind and neighborly and doing good as opportunity arises—which is well enough in its way and which was never more needed than now, but it is certainly not basic Christianity. For Protestantism in America, despite a steady increase in church membership and vastly improved opportunities of religious education, religious illiteracy—the words are not too strong—constitutes a first-class problem: multitudes uninformed and misinformed, lost in a wilderness of laissez-faire thinking, having broken with the beliefs of an earlier day, with nothing to put in their place, at any rate nothing as positive and vital, so that when they are asked what they believe, they fall back on impressions absorbed in childhood or repeat vague generalities rather than offer anything in the nature of a clear-cut credo. Here are the replies of three persons classing themselves as Christians, to the question, Do you believe there is a God? "Oh, yes, I believe there is. But whether I have just been brought up to believe it as a child, I don't know." "Well, I've always been brought up to believe, but you do wonder sometimes. I don't think I can argue on it." "I couldn't say, we are only told there is one, and I suppose we must believe in one."

What such vagueness means for active, intelligent, mature church membership is only too obvious. It turns out men and women who have no star to steer by, no center for thought, no incentive to action. They have no creed, no passionate attachment which wakens their enthusiasm, rouses their devotion and loyalty, and sweeps them off their feet. As another has put it: "They have a pew in some church and if it is not too fine, or again not too wet, they will be there. No one can say they are against Jesus Christ. It would be just not true. But on the other hand, they are not hot for him, not absorbed in his cause, not enthusiastic to help him, not almost one-ideaed about this thing as many people are about football, or art, or business, or whatever makes life for them. Always when they speak of him it is with grave respect; often they do a little for him; but nothing that spells sacrifice, that pushes them out from the center of their lives, that upsets their own comforts, that means giving up anything they really want. They are mildly Christians, but not very much." Isn't that the story of most of us?

> *What would I burn for, and whom not spare?*
> *I who have faith in an easy chair.*

And it all runs back in the end to the absence in us of the quality so apparent in Christians in every forward-moving epoch of the church's history—the absence of personal conviction, rooted and grounded in immediate, self-authenticating experience.

All of which brings me to another mark of a living church. A sense of conviction always issues *in a sense of vocation.* Whoever genuinely believes anything becomes a propagandist. If you believe a certain medicine is effective, you will make it your business to recommend it to others. If you believe a certain political theory, practically applied, is likely to work out for the greatest happiness of the greatest number, and the belief and the welfare of humanity really count for something with you, then you will conceive it to be your first task to win others to its support. Whatever you may think of the content of Peter Howard's book you cannot question the aptness and soundness of its title—*Ideas Have Legs.* Indeed they have—long, strong legs. See to what lengths they carried Hitler and the German people, with the whole world in consequence involved in a maelstrom. See what a revolution they are working in Russia, and not only in Russia but far beyond it, for communism is the most aggressive missionary movement of our time. Its representatives have made the world their parish and display a devotion, a venturesomeness, a courage that compel self-examination. Said Radek, at one time the chief of propaganda in Moscow, "This Communism, you see, is a religion. Our young men must preach its gospel. They are willing to die for it." There you have the very thing for which I am pleading—a sense of conviction issuing in a sense of vocation.

At its best, Christianity has always had it. "Necessity is laid upon me. Woe to me if I do not preach the gospel!" It is the cry that accounts for the missionary journeys of Paul and the establishment of the church in Asia Minor and Europe. "Here I stand: I can do no other." It is the declaration of Luther at the Diet of Worms—daring, defiant, uncompromising, final: the declaration of a man with a tremendous sense of mission.

I will not be a liar. I will speak in season and out of season. I will not take counsel with flesh and blood, and flatter myself with the dream that, while every man on earth back to Abel who ever tried to testify against the world has been laughed at, misunderstood, slandered, and that—bitterest of all—by the very people he loved, I am alone to escape. My path is clear and I will follow in it. He who died for me and who gave me you, shall I not trust him through whatever new and strange paths he may lead me?

It is Charles Kingsley's letter to his wife when his forthright teaching and preaching involved him in a turmoil of bitter controversy and strife and when friends and relatives pleaded with him to "put the tongue of discretion in the cheek of propriety." There is tension in it, too much tension. It would have helped Kingsley if he could have relaxed more than he did. But the strength of conviction and the sense of mission leap at us from every sentence.

Ideas have legs. The fires that kindled the heroes of the faith, the thing that churned their souls and kept them toiling on in the teeth of obstacles, apparently insuperable, was an idea, nay rather an ideal, an ideal which had become incarnate in Christ. It gave them a cause in which they fervently believed and which sent them out in joyous and deliberate abandon as on a crusade. In 1830 Benjamin Constant, the French philosopher, received a message at the hands of his friends in Paris who were overthrowing the Bourbons. "A terrible game is being played here: our heads are in danger: come and add yours." That was the appeal of Christ to his followers. What we need in the church now is the same crusading spirit for, to quote Berdyaev once more, these are times when "Christianity is going back to the state she enjoyed before Constantine; she has to undertake the conquest of the world afresh." She will never do it unless her members are animated by a devotion to their cause no less passionate than Hitler felt for his and the Communists feel for theirs. She will never do it until she is less timid, cautious and compromising and far more venturesome and aggressive. She will never do it until her leaders, instead of drawing up pious, platitudinous resolutions about which everybody can agree, go in for courageous thinking and plain, candid speaking. She will never do it until the rank and file of her members know what they believe and why, and have for their master motive the dissemination of their faith the world over.

Years ago in Boston Bishop F. J. McConnell delivered a speech, the memory of which is still treasured. He said:

During the Boxer Rebellion hundreds, probably thousands of Chinese Christians were martyred. There they knelt, with their heads on the blocks, the knives trembling in the hands of their executioners. All they needed to do was to grunt out a Chinese word that meant "I recant" and their lives would be saved. Now, what should I have done under these circumstances? And I speak not simply personally, but in a repre-sentative capacity, for I think the rest of you are very much like myself. With my head on the block I suspect I should have said, "Hold on! I think I can make a statement that will be satisfactory to all sides."

For too long, Christians have been like that, accommodating, worldly-wise, pliable, acquiescing in what is conventional, leaving their unbelieving neighbors uncertain as to what the church stands for, unless it is an easygoing toleration of things as they are, with mild desire that they may grow better in time, so far as that is compatible with the maintenance of vested interests. Salt, light, leaven—those were the terms Jesus used in envisaging the impact of his disciples on the world. And today, the greatest danger confronting the church is not that it will die. The church will not die. The ever-present danger which confronts the church is that it may become insipid—standing for nothing in particular, hesitant, halfhearted, its message muffled and uncertain.

How is that to be prevented? How in point of fact has it been prevented? When has the church been like salt and light and leaven, its influence potent, its temper militant? Not alone when its members have had robust convictions and an overpowering sense of divine election but when they have been *in close, intimate daily touch with Christ, their Savior and Master.* "I know whom I have believed," cried Paul. Not what but whom. Ideas have legs but men, if they are to be stirred to action, must have more than ideas. Ideas, like ideals, are poor ghosts until they become incarnate. Back of the idea is the person animating it. Back of the movement is the leader directing and inspiring it—Buddha, Mahomet, Napoleon, Lenin, Hitler, Gandhi, Christ. Certainly Christ had no compunction in attaching men to himself. He taught them to yield their faith to him, and in generation after generation that is what thousands upon thousands have done. He has become the object of their faith, their Law, their Light, their Leader, their Lord. It is he who has inspired their sense of conviction. It is from him they have caught the sense of vocation. Under the constraint born of association with him they have gone forth as on a great venture to labor for the kingdom of God. He has given them, to quote David Christie, a world they can live in, a cause they can live for, a self they can live with, a Master they can die for. They have brought life to the church and help and healing to the world.

Where in such matters as these do we stand? The question is a personal one and must be personally answered. One thing I know. If today you and I make a fresh, or a first, dedication of our lives to

The Marks of a Living Church

Christ, resolve to serve his cause with the same ardor and intensity of devotion that others give to the service of causes far less worthy and deserving, the winds of God will blow through this church and we shall see his mighty acts done in our midst and far beyond it.

September 28, 1947

Love or Perish!

THE CHRISTIAN FAITH from generation to generation makes a powerful appeal to the minds and emotions of men. It does so because it stands for the truth at the heart of things, that God is love, that love is not a weak sentiment but the profoundest practical need of mankind. Everywhere people are hungering for it as they hunger for food. What the law of gravity is to the sun and the stars, love is to men and women. It is the groundwork of human existence and the life-principle of society.

And yet—this is the paradox—more and more we are relying on force, not love. We are making the world into an arsenal. We are bolstering up our way of life on the crude doctrine of the survival of the strongest, as though we believed that the first and last thing to be said about the world is that it is a hard world and that to survive in it we must be hard. Is this what we really believe—that force, not love, is the groundwork of human existence and the life-principle of human society? It is a belief that makes short shrift of Christ and the Christian faith.

Consider the direction in which the world is moving. We have known for fifty years that there is enough energy in a handful of dirt to blow up a metropolis, but we persist in the effort to find ever more effective ways to release it. We have been horrified so often by descriptions of what would happen if a hydrogen bomb were to be dropped on any of our big cities that we do not shudder as we should shudder when we are told that during a test a hydrogen bomb obliterated a whole island. At a fatal moment, the use of such bombs could produce an incalculable and irretrievable holocaust. We are living from day to day under the threat of a two-way bomb war that could destroy the whole fabric of civilization and even imperil the existence of the human race.

Since the Korean War we in the United States have spent billions to preserve our national security. Yet, on any showing, our position throughout the world is less secure now than it was a few years ago. The arms bill of the Western world runs today at approximately $100 billion a year. A mere one percent of that sum invested in India's five-year-plan would increase the effectiveness of that country's modernization by 100 percent and set it far ahead of China, its Communist competitor. Is the only possible answer to the political threat of communism fear, hostility, superior military might? Ought we not to turn back from the suicidal path we are following? I say "suicidal," for the perfection of weapons of wholesale destruction and extermination is irrational, immoral, dangerous to national security, inimical to life itself. I say "suicidal" because when the first atomic bomb was dropped over Hiroshima it destroyed 60 percent of all the houses in a city of 318,000 people, and damaged practically all the rest. That single bomb killed between 53,000 and 80,000 people. And it was only an atomic bomb! Think of the destruction a hydrogen bomb would create.

But, it will be said, what alternative have we? Are we to submit supinely to Communist totalitarianism? Surely there is another alternative, and Christians should be foremost in commending it, in calling for a stop to irrational measures that are automatically bringing us close to a final catastrophe. The other alternative is a policy of working steadily toward justice and cooperation and free intercourse with all peoples, in the faith that love begets love as certainly as hatred begets hatred. This is the alternative to which Christians are committed—that God is love, that love is the groundwork of human existence and the life-principle of society, that the human heart is everywhere the same, and love is the way to it. Those who dismiss this as too idealistic for human nature and international relations as they know them, as impractical and therefore irrelevant, need to do two things. They need to think a bit more about the essential meaning of the Christian faith, and they need to take another look at the direction in which the world is moving. When they say that love won't work in a world like this they ought to face the question whether the hard, unsentimental principle of the survival of the strongest is working. Did it work in the case of Hitler? Did it work in the case of Stalin? Will it work in Algeria? Will it work in South Africa? Out of the thunder of contemporary events one fact is emerging: The obligation of humanity is to live by the law of love if it is to live at all. That is the alternative: love or perish!

Christian preachers are not alone in saying this, though even if they were solitary voices it would still be their duty to speak out. There are *humanists* who are saying this. Lewis Mumford is one of them. He says:

Let us deal with our own massive sins and errors as a step towards establishing firm relations of confidence with the rest of mankind. And let us, first of all, have the courage to speak up on behalf of humanity, on behalf of civilization, on behalf of life itself against the methodology of barbarism to which we are now committed. If as a reaction we have become mad it is time for the world to take note of that madness. If we are still human and sane, then it is time for the powerful voice of sanity to be heard once more in our land.

There are *scientists* making the same emphasis. Dr. J. Robert Oppenheimer was invited to deliver a nationwide broadcast marking the end of Columbia University's year-long bicentennial celebration. The newspapers at the time reported that in his address he "set a path for mankind" and "outlined his philosophy for a changing world." Here is how the address finished.

This cannot be an easy life. We shall have a rugged time of it to keep our minds open and to keep them deep . . . in a great open windy world; but this is, as I see it, the condition of man; and in this condition we can help, because we can love one another.

Think of it! The one-time head of the Los Alamos atomic project exhorting world strugglers to "love one another."

Isn't something like this the burden of what many postwar novelists are saying, such novelists as Carson McCullers, Alan Paton,

Love or Perish!

Richard Ellison? In their fiction, love has a special character and urgency. It is the only recourse against frustration and isolation, against a terrifying sense of meaninglessness. The only way to define and discover the self is to get beyond the self through love. Without this, in a time of unstable values and totalitarian ideologies, human impulses are likely to be violent, predatory and destructive. The stress is on communication through communion. There is a reaction against totally political solutions. What one novelist after another is saying is that simple human affection is all that can now be counted upon, what they are saying is that without love too much of life and life's meaning is lost.

Love or perish! For years now this is what *psychologists* have been telling us, Suttie and Menninger and Fromm and Freud. Love is not just a matter of religious idealism. It is the indispensable emotion. Men and nations can no more live without it than they can live without breathing. The last half century has brought insights and discoveries in the psychology of love and hate that are in their way just as startling as the discoveries of modern physics. It is a strange historical coincidence that during the years when man learned to unchain the destructive forces inherent in matter he learned also more than ever about the nature of destructiveness within himself. He has learned that hate, fear, resentment, hostility work like poisons, that they literally affect the secretions of the body and induce disease. In an age when man has brought his powers of subduing nature to such a pitch that by using them he could easily exterminate life, he has learned that love is the indispensable emotion, that his need of it is as deep as his need for food, that he sentences himself to frustration and self-destruction when he scorns it, when he hates and quarrels and will not live in peace and goodwill with his fellows.

A missionary in Africa whose wife had died on the mission field was furloughed home. Together with his small son he set out, first by wagon over bumpy paths and roads, then by steamer. On the ocean rough weather was encountered, and the boat began to pitch and roll. "Daddy," the boy asked, "when will we have a home that will not shake?" That boy was making a query for the whole human race. And the testimony that comes from scientists, novelists, psychologists is that man is sinning against the very nature of things when he lives without love. He is hungry for it and frustrated and unhappy without it. It is the greatest thing he knows. It is the one essential vitamin of the soul. It is the ultimate meaning of life. It is the stable element in an unstable world. A poem called *Ultimatum* by Peggy Pond Church states the case:

Now the frontiers are all closed.
There is no other country we can run away to.
There is no ocean we can cross over.
At last we must turn and live with one another.
We cannot escape this day any longer.
We cannot continue to choose between good and evil
  (the good for ourselves, the evil for our neighbors);
We must all bear the equal burden.
At last we who have been running away must turn and face it.
There is no room for hate left in the world we must live in.
Now we must learn love. We can no longer escape it.
We can no longer escape from one another.
Love is no longer a theme for eloquence, or a way of
  life for a few to choose whose hearts can decide it.
It is the sternest necessity; the unequivocal ultimatum.
There is no other way out; there is no country we can flee to.
There is no man on earth who must not face this task now.

And so I come back to the point from which I started. The Christian faith makes an irresistible appeal to us because it meets a deep need of our nature. It revives hopes that were born long ago with Christ in Bethlehem and that have never died. It stands for the truth at the heart of things, that love is *the* attribute of the Power behind the universe, that God is love, and therefore that love is the groundwork of human existence and the life-principle of society. We are so made that if we do not love we perish. It was this that Jesus came to make known. After he lived and died in it, the world was never the same again. A new and spiritual energy entered into the process of human life. It is not exhausted. It will never be exhausted. Sooner or later force bows before gentleness, and love is seen to be stronger than hate. As the apostle Paul expressed it, "Love can outlast anything. It is, in fact, the one thing that still stands when all else has fallen."

December 23, 1956

The Inevitableness of Easter

"It could not be that death should keep him in its grip [Acts 2:24, NEB]."

PETER, WHO SAID that, had not always thought it. Nor had his fellow disciples for whom he was the spokesman. They had followed Jesus to Jerusalem, and had been gratified by the homage shown him by the crowds. True, he had spoken ominous words about his approaching death, but the triumphal entry to the capital city and their confidence in his messianic claims had left little room for foreboding. Then all at once catastrophe was upon them. He was arrested, condemned, crucified. Their behavior in the crisis was pitiful. Judas had betrayed him, Peter denied him, the rest forsook him and fled.

If we had been in their shoes, wouldn't we have done the same? They had looked to him for emancipation from Rome, and Rome had put an end to him. It had seemed to them as though God himself had endorsed the verdict of Caiaphas and Pilate, and by permitting Jesus to die on the cross had placed on him the stigma of his own curse. For the Law had said, "Cursed is every one that hangeth on a tree," and to the pious Jew the curse of the Law was God's verdict, from which there could be no appeal. Who were they to let their memories of the Master, the impression he had made on them by the purity of his life, the power of his teaching, the wonder of his works, stand for one moment against the unmistakable sentence of God? What was there for them to do, their hopes shattered, but to forget all that had happened—or try to—go back home, and pick up the threads of the old life?

Then came the astounding experience of Easter morning. Christ crucified, dead and buried, had risen from the grave. The tomb was empty. Death had not vanquished him; he had vanquished it. What clinched the matter for them, bred certitude in them, was his actual appearance—to Mary, to Peter, to James, to the apostles, to Thomas, to the two disciples on the road to Emmaus, to five hundred disciples at once. As more and more evidence was afforded them, bewilderment gave way to exhilaration. The face of the world was changed for them. The fact of the resurrection took fire in their souls and utterly transformed them. No longer was there any talk of going home, for Jesus was not a lost leader but a living, present reality. Reunited in fellowship with him they went out on the streets to make known the great good news that he was still living, still guiding, still at work in the world.

Within a few weeks they wondered that they could ever have believed anything else. In retrospect they saw clearly that what had happened, in the very nature of the case, in God's world, was bound to happen. It was inevitable; any other sequence of events would have been inconceivable. Their Master—the Pioneer of Life they had begun to call him—was not the person to be subdued and overcome by death. He had passed through it, blazing a trail, carrying the frontiers with him, bringing back the title-deeds. A life like his, a mind, spirit, character like his, could never have ended at the grave in defeat and extinction. This was what Peter standing up with the eleven maintained on the day of Pentecost: "It could not be that death should keep him in its grip [NEB]."

Isn't this our conviction also? What does Easter mean to you? Surely more than the perpetuation of a great memory, more than reverence for the noblest soul that ever breathed, more than a sanctified kind of hero-worship. Think about Jesus. He is absolutely unprecedented, far and away the most significant person the world has known. As Lecky the historian wrote, he did more "in three short years to regenerate and soften mankind than all the disquisitions of philosophers and all the exhortations of moralists."

The Inevitableness of Easter

Thou seemst both human and divine,
The highest, holiest manhood Thou.

This is the Christian conviction. It is incongruous, incredible as well as incongruous, to think of Christ as crucified, dead and buried—period; at the mercy of an indignity done to his body, swept at death into nothingness, Good Friday really Black Friday, a gibbet on Golgotha the last, the final chapter in his story. Who can believe that? Who can make sense of that? On this Easter morning don't we say what Peter did? "It could not be that death should keep him in its grip [NEB]."

Why, even for those who fall short of the moral and spiritual stature of Christ, we make a similar claim. That death is not the end is an old and persistent belief, sociologists telling us that it is more widespread even than belief in a God or gods. At their best men and women find it difficult to reconcile themselves to the theory that they were made to live their life, do their work, and then rot in the grave. If a person, in Dr. Fosdick's phrase, becomes a real person, grows with the years, grows in wisdom, strength of character, grace of personality, is full of good works, it doesn't make sense to think of death blotting him out. Even though his influence lives on after he has gone, it still doesn't make sense—Plato's *Phaedo,* but no Plato, Handel's "Hallelujah Chorus" but no Handel, Lincoln's Gettysburg speech but no Lincoln, Thomas Dooley's hospital in Laos but no Thomas Dooley. George Herbert Palmer needed no one to tell him that his wife's influence would live on long after she had gone, but about her passing he wrote:

Though no regrets are proper for the manner of her death, who can contemplate the fact of it and not call the world irrational, if out of deference to a few particles of disordered matter it excludes so fair a spirit?

Doesn't your mind work in the same way? Don't you make the same sort of instinctive demand? At Easter we fall to thinking of the best souls we have known, "loved long since and lost awhile." Do that. Recall the gifts and graces that drew you to them, the faithful hearts and strong intelligences that won your admiration and affection. Can you resign yourself to the belief that all is over with them, that the bright spirit that burned in them has forever been extinguished, so much courage, so much endurance, so much faith, so much affection, so much sweetness vanished as a bubble? Don't you say the very thing Peter said? It could not be that death should keep them in its grip. What tremendous force, then, the conviction has when applied to Christ! The noblest life of which history has any record could not have come to a full stop at Calvary. The crucifixion was not the last, the final chapter in Christ's story. "God raised him from the dead."

More is at stake here than personal survival after death. Also at issue is the question: What kind of world do we live in? Is this a spiritual universe? Is it under the control of a God of righteousness and justice? Is it rooted and grounded on moral foundations? Or is human history merely a scramble for wealth and power? Is the story of humanity the story of a long procession of sufferers, for whose suffering there is no justification and will be no ultimate vindication? All the religions of the world notwithstanding, is that the fact of the matter? Are Communists right when they deny that there is anything above or beyond or outlasting the natural order of which we form a part? Where does the final word lie—with love, goodness and truth or with hate, evil and error?

This is the ultimate question and the resurrection is the answer. It stands for more than the assurance of personal survival after death; it has cosmic significance. If a life like the life of Jesus vanished as a bubble, if all that nobility was utterly at the mercy of the wickedness of men, virtue trampled on, goodness mocked, the last word with Caiaphas and Pilate, how is it possible to believe in God or a kingdom of God? You have on your hands a riddle to which there is no clue. You are shut up to the conclusion that the forces in which evil roots are more powerful than the forces of goodness—truth on the scaffold, wrong on the throne, no God within the shadows keeping watch above his own. It is a dismal, dreary conclusion. We are asked to believe that we live in a world where there is air for the lungs and food for the stomach but no answer to the deepest hungers of the soul. We are asked to believe that we live in a world where the race is to the swift and the battle to the strong, and where faith and hope and love disappear as if they had never been. When a person sees life thus, subscribes to the dictum of Bertrand Russell that "on man and all his race the slow, sure doom falls pitiless and dark," all he has to sustain him is the courage of his own stoicism.

See, by contrast, what the Easter faith affirms. Death did not keep Jesus in its grip. The cause to which he devoted himself did not go down to defeat. The last word was not with Caiaphas or Pilate. What an appalling thing it would be if we lived in a world where the Neros and the Napoleons, the Hitlers and the Stalins had the last word, where hatred and lies and wickedness were supreme, our best loves and loyalties—like ourselves—poured through a hole at the heart of things and lost. We do not live in such a world. There are spiritual forces at work which set sharp limits to man's will to power, against which all violators of the moral order pit themselves in vain. Life will work out only one way, God's way. If a man, a nation, a civilization chooses a different way, however stable it may appear for a time, if it is not God's way, if it flouts his moral order, it will lead inexorably to decline and disaster. Easter comes year by year as a reminder that this is God's world. There is a Power at work behind the universe which is on the side of goodness, truth and love. Jesus, who all his life staked everything on God, did not trust in him in vain. We associate Easter with the assurance of immortality but there is a still greater assurance. The resurrection strengthens our faith that there is an eternal order of righteousness and that the universe at its heart is spiritual. "Thine is the kingdom and the power and the glory forever, Amen."

What, personally, do you make of all this? Churches are thronged at Easter. People attend then who do not put in an appearance at any other time of the year. One wonders why. The cynic thinks the Easter festival is a fashion parade. Force of habit has certainly a great deal to do with it. One of our magazines carried a cartoon of a clergyman addressing an overflow congregation on Easter Sunday and asking, "Are you not just a little curious as to what goes on here between Easters?" Regardless of the motivation, what does Easter mean to you? Or rather, what does Christ mean to you? Do you reckon him a notable historical personage like Socrates, Buddha, Gandhi? Do you reverence him as the sublimest ethical teacher of all time? Or do you believe that he overcame the sharpness of death, that is to say, he is not only the Jesus of history but the Jesus of experience, alive and at work in the world here and now? If you incline to shy away from that last question, dismissing it perhaps as sheer mysticism, take another look at the facts. Christianity is something more than hero-worship. It is not just the perpetuation of a great memory.

It is a relationship to and a fellowship with a Christ who is "alive for evermore." Everything in Christianity depends on the reality of the resurrection of Christ, on the fact that he rose from the grave, appeared to his disciples, made his presence felt in their lives, *and still makes his presence felt,* is in our generation as great an actuality as he was to his first followers.

"Shall I tell you," David Livingstone asked the students of Glasgow University on his return from sixteen years spent in Africa, "what sustained me amidst the toil and hardship, and loneliness of my exiled life? It was the promise, 'Lo, I am with you always, even unto the end.' " For multitudes this is life's most precious conviction. When they speak about Christ, they use not only the past and future tenses but the present tense as well. He is not only a great memory and a great hope, he is the Eternal Contemporary, offering the same transforming friendship today that he offered to Mary and Peter and John and Paul long ago.

> *No more in Galilee we look for Thee,*
> *O Risen Lord;*
> *In every land and on each moonlit sea*
> *Thy voice is heard;*
> *And when Thy saints are gathered in Thy Name,*
> *Closer Thou art to each than fire to flame.*

"Lo, I am with you always." That is the heartwarming, heart-gladdening fact we celebrate this morning. Jesus Christ is a living present reality. "It could not be that death should keep him in its grip [NEB]." "Hallelujah! For the Lord God Omnipotent reigneth."

April 2, 1961

Ernest T. Campbell

Preaching Minister of The Riverside Church

1968–1976

The aim of preaching is to get people to say "yes" or "no" to something that matters. Unlike a classroom lecture, it is verdict-oriented. And, wonder of wonders, through such "foolishness" God works!
—Ernest T. Campbell

Experience, Expectation and Surprise

TOWARD THE END of Christopher Fry's play *The Lady's Not for Burning,* one finds this disquieting exchange:

Margaret says, "Have any of you seen that poor child Alizon? I think she must be lost."

Nicholas answers, "Who isn't? The best thing we can do is to make wherever we're lost in look as much like home as we can. Now don't be worried. She can't be more lost than she was with us."

"The best thing we can do is to make wherever we're lost in look as much like home as we can." To minimize our alienation and make sense of life is a concern to which we give ourselves all our days. There is a lot of reality out there to be reckoned with; a bewildering assortment of values from which to choose; an obstacle course to manage; a sizable amount of chaos on which to impose some order; a network of systems that calls for resistance or compliance. And we have to do this reckoning, choosing, managing, ordering, resisting and complying with a self that is housed in a vulnerable body—a heartbeat away from death—and within a span of time that at its longest is all too short!

Two resources have been given us with which to cope: These are experience and expectation. With all due respect to the existentialists, without experience and expectation none of us could live!

Experience, Expectation and Surprise

Experience is the word we use to denote a remembered past. Fortunately all the ground we break is not fresh. We stand on the shoulders of our predecessors. Each generation does not have to discover anew the law of gravity or the light bulb.

In a broader sense the lessons of history are there to illumine our understanding. The graffiti on Belshazzar's wall holds truth for nations in the present, as do the death of Socrates, the ovens of Dachau or Belsen, and the Bay of Pigs.

Not only so, but we carry with us the lessons of our own personal history. Day by day, thank God, we are not called upon to break fresh ground. It is amazing, when one thinks on it, how often some remembered circumstance rises up to influence our conduct in the present.

Back when I was in college in the Roosevelt years (that's Franklin, not Theodore) I had a roommate with whom I shared a washbasin. We worked it out pretty well. He always shaved ahead of me in the mornings, for which I had other advantages later on in the day. One morning Earl proceeded to shave. He was in a hurry. There was studying to do and exam time was coming. After he had finished scraping off his growth, he placed the razor down on the basin and bent over to rinse his face in cold water. As he reached for the faucet his finger slid right into the open face of the razor. An enormous gash developed that streaked the basin with blood. To this day, wherever I shave I never lay my razor on the surface of the basin. Experience!

Remembered bouts with indigestion monitor the food we eat. The consequences of a loss of temper urge us in the direction of a more patient nature. Recollections of former intimacies with God come back to haunt our slackness in religion. This is experience. We build upon the past. Those who will not learn the lessons of the past are bound to repeat its mistakes. Repeat situations keep coming up. Yesterday can help us now.

But joined to experience is the other faculty, called expectation. We can recall the past, we can also project a future. We know that certain courses will lead to predictable ends. The Club of Rome, for example, extrapolated a future for the world from present tendencies.

This also happens on a lesser scale in our personal biographies. So many years in school, then a degree and a job. So many dollars set aside each week, then money enough for a car. So many weeks of careful dieting, then a healthier and more attractive body. So many hours at the keyboard, then competence with the piano. So much time with God each day, then a surer spiritual discernment. Without our expectations we would be as good as dead! The present would entomb us! The curtain might just as well fall.

Experience and expectation enable us to live. Some of us lean more to experience. That is, we tend to be past-oriented. I can't tell you how many meetings I've been in where some new proposal was defeated on one of two grounds: We did it before, or we never did it before. The older we get the more we tend to rely on experience.

Others of us are given more to expectation. This is largely true of the young who prefer experimentation to experience. This accounts, in part at least, for the enormous tensions that we feel between the generations.

In a viable society both are necessary. All experience and no expectation would produce a cautious dullness. All expectation and no experience would issue in a fatal recklessness. Experience and expectation.

Biblical faith goes beyond both! This is the burden of my word to you today. Biblical faith goes beyond both and adds to life *the element of surprise!* Experience rests on memory, expectation rests on calculation, but surprise is nourished by faith and becomes the ground of hope.

Read the Bible again, this time with the throttle of your imagination wide open, and it will astound you how many surprises are packed among its pages. History is more than repetition, because God's new keeps breaking in. History is more than calculation, for more than could ever have been expected has happened and keeps happening today.

Israel itself is a surprise among the nations. Abraham is ninety-nine years old. His wife is well past child-bearing age. The patriarch is drifting and yawning his way through an unwanted retirement beneath the oaks of Mamre. One day he looks up and sees three men go by. Desperate for company, he invites them in and offers them hospitality.

One of the three turns to Abraham rather boldly and asks, "Where is your wife?" Abraham replies, "What kind of place do you think this is? She's in the back in the kitchen." The man undaunted says, "She's going to become pregnant!" At this point there is laughter in the kitchen. Sarah has been listening in. When the visitors leave, God says to Abraham, "Why did Sarah laugh and ask, 'Shall I indeed bear a child now that I am old?' Is anything too hard for God?" Then just three chapters further on, we read that "the Lord did to Sarah as he had said and Sarah conceived and bore Abraham a son in his old age." Surprise!! Isaac is born and the promise is vouchsafed.

A tiny minority, Israel's future is aborted by captivity in Egypt. Egypt has all the guns, all the money, all the power—enough to enslave these people forever. Then surprise! God calls an "audible" at the Red Sea and commands Moses to go through center. And he does.

David goes out against Goliath. Experience says that the lad should at least be properly attired, so Saul's armor is provided. David graciously rejects the conventional equipment of battle and, surprise, the giant falls!

Israel has always lived, and lives today, in an environment of hostility—larger nations that could, at least on paper, swallow her up. We describe Israel as extending from Dan to Beersheba. When I first learned those two extension points of the kingdom my mind imagined a vast expanse. But Dan to Beersheba is a mere 150 miles. A minister would drive it in three hours and a layperson in two! It was no bigger than the size of Wales. Feature that! Yet Israel survives. And she serves as the carrier of promise. This has to be one of the choice surprises of the world!

And on it goes. A man is born to obscure parents in a backwoods province and becomes the most unforgettable character ever to walk the stage of history. His closest followers are nondescript, yet they rise up and turn the world upside down. Surprise! We never would have thought it. He is soon put to death on an instrument of shame, but that cross becomes a cherished symbol of invincible love. Surprise! Surprise!

Always the surprises come. While the enlightened pagans are looking at the observable facts, God moves in to surprise. Who would have thought that an unimpressive wisp of a man, clad in a loincloth and carrying a bamboo stock, would be the one to set India free from foreign domination? What a surprise!

Who would have thought that a tired Negro woman pressing for a seat on an Alabama bus would ignite a social revolution? Surprise!

Who would have thought that the most powerful nation in the world would come a cropper in the rice paddies of Vietnam? Surprise!

Who would have thought that a policeman in Washington, D.C., noticing a strip of tape across the lock of a door in a new development, would unseat a President and change the face of history? Surprise!

Beyond experience and beyond expectation, surprises come. This is why Regis Debray is moved to say that, "Perhaps a new law—or anti-law—of history will have to be invented: the law of surprises. Whenever anything important happens in history it is always by surprise."

Whence come such surprises? They are the doings of the Lord! That's it. They are the doings of the Lord. Another is at work. They are signs of what the Bible calls the kingdom of God—that kingdom which is featured in the prayer that teaches us to pray, "Thy kingdom come." So Jesus said to the Pharisees, "The kingdom of God is not coming with signs to be observed; nor will they say, 'Lo, here it is!' or 'There!' for behold, the kingdom of God is in the midst of you."

It is not observable. That is, it cannot be extrapolated from the facts of the present. If that were the case the kingdom would be confused with the humanist concept of progress. It cannot be seized. It cannot be ideologized. It cannot be captured by a party, or a nation, or a system. Nobody can say, "lo here, lo there," "he's got it," "she's got it," "I've got it." But it is real. It is made up of fresh starts, surprising turns, strange twists and innovations. Just when we think we have things figured out and have exalted common sense to a science, surprise! And the whole thing falls.

The kingdom of God is "in the midst of you" not "within you" as the King James Version has it. The kingdom is not a mystical inner state. We are talking about *a state of affairs,* not *a state of mind.* One always gets uneasy when ballroom religions talk about the God in you. Jesus never asked folks to let the kingdom into their hearts. He summoned them to enter the kingdom. It is a reality, this kingdom, not a psychological condition. It is in the midst of us, that is, it is within the world we know. We cannot always see it because of our fixation with experience and expectation.

God's surprises blow our minds. They are not like anything we have known or anything that we can easily prognosticate. Leave some room for God. The kingdom is mostly hidden at the moment. Its fullness has not yet dawned. It is both here and coming.

These surprises occur not only in the world-at-large but also in individual experience. I don't have to tell you that. You have walked past enough surprises to know what I am saying. The kingdom is local as well as universal.

One of our problems today is that we are overly influenced by two sciences that deal primarily with *life as it is:* sociology and psychiatry. I have no quarrel with either. But the gospel has to do with *life as it might become.* And you can study "what is" so much that you lose the ability to envision a better future. Experience and expectation become the railings to which we desperately cling. God is trying to shake our hands loose and alert us to the surprises.

Why, before this day is ended God could knock you off your feet! Something you read or hear. Some new person entering your life. Some experience of failure or success. Some prayer uttered in a moment of sheer exhaustion. An unwelcome illness or enforced idleness. *You may be finished with yourself but God isn't.*

This kingdom does not come with observable signs. You cannot control it. Nor will it ever be yours to say, "lo here" or "lo there," for behold this kingdom is in the midst of you. As you contemplate your future do not fail to factor in the kingdom! God is still on the premises, impelled by a creative, restless love. Somewhere, somehow when you least expect anything good to happen, God may *stop you in your tracks, turn you completely around and start you in a new direction.* That's what faith is about. It moves beyond experience and expectation to surprise.

Surprises are impossible, you say. I answer, yes. But only the impossible is sure because it belongs to God!

July 20, 1975

Overheard in Room 738

BILL KNOWLES WAS a sturdy young man of thirty-two years
—a schoolteacher by choice but at the moment a patient in hospital
definitely *not* by choice. His skis had done him in. Attempting a ski
slope too steep for his experience he slammed into a tree and shattered
something in his right hip.

Five hours later—after a painful ambulance ride and what
seemed like an endless series of X rays, after the welcome anesthetic
and more than two and a half hours on the operating table, Bill was
wheeled into Room 738 on the orthopedic floor of Good Samaritan
Hospital.

He wasn't exactly "cover material" for a health magazine! His
face had been scratched up pretty badly in the fall. Besides, caught
without pajamas of his own, he found himself modeling one of those
ghastly "one-size-fits-all" shapeless white gowns that hospitals throw
in as part of the deal for your hundred dollars a day.

Uncomfortably immobilized by an imprisoning cast, and bitter
at the remembrance of the day's events, Bill eagerly swallowed the
sedative given him as evening fell and soon was lost in sleep.

Morning comes quickly in hospitals. Even though it was tunnel-
dark outside, Bill was awakened by the rattle of trays and dishes.

Instinctively he pulled on the base of the metal triangle hanging above his head and maneuvered into a sit-up position.

For the first time since his arrival Bill noticed that he had a roommate. To his right by the window, a position in hospitals that connotes seniority, was a man some ten years older than himself. It was clear that his need to be there centered in a damaged left ankle.

"Hi," said Bill. "My name is Knowles, Bill Knowles. Hope I didn't keep you awake last night with my snoring."

"Not at all," said his roomie. "A couple of doctors were in checking on your chart but that was it. My name is Chris, Chris Moore. I'm glad to meet you. This is my second week. Compound fracture. Happened down at work when a case of tire irons fell off a truck and got me smack on the bone."

Through breakfast and beyond, the two filled each other in on who they were: how they felt about Watergate, inflation and the gasoline shortage; what they thought of Muhammad Ali's recent victory over Joe Frazier.

They had succeeded in putting a good beginning on their friendship when a well-muscled young man clad in hospital white from head to toe came in and proceeded to give both Chris and Bill a combination bath and rubdown.

In the afterglow of this welcome treatment, Bill turned to his newfound friend and, as much to make conversation as anything, said, "Hey, what's with the male nurse bit? I feel cheated. Like I do on an airplane when I get a man steward instead of one of those cute stewardesses they're always showing in the ads."

"Careful, buddy," chirped Chris. "Your male chauvinism is showing. What you're really trying to say"—and he lowered his voice as he went on—"what you're really trying to say is that any guy who would take a job like that is probably a queer."

No, that wasn't what Bill was about at all. And he felt uncomfortable with the turn the subject had taken. First the hip and now this—forced to room with a small-town "hard hat"!

He couldn't let the matter stand. Having counseled high school students for years, he knew that human sexuality was a subject that required care and sensitivity.

"Look," he said, forgetting the miseries of his hip as he warmed to the challenge, "guys can become nurses for a variety of reasons.

Women can fly airplanes and run track, and men can be secretaries and nurses. Good ones too!

"Besides, if a guy happens to be a homosexual, what's so wrong with that?"

Chris was willing to concede that men and women could do a lot of role switching in society. There was something about that in the papers almost every day. But he felt a surge of resentment with Bill's question, "Being a homosexual, what's so wrong with that?" It was his turn to dig in.

"Are you defending the gays?" he asked. "You told me just minutes ago that you have a wife and two sons. Would you want those kids to get mixed up with a pervert when they're old enough to join the 'Y' or go off to a summer camp? Listen, I've got no time for those phonies. One of them made a pass at me when I was fifteen and I almost killed him."

Bill twisted over on his side for a sip of water and settled back to continue a discussion that had become rather heated. "You've got no right to judge all homosexuals by the relatively few who happen to be predators. Gays are as resentful of the proselyting homosexual as you and I are of the heterosexual guy who can't keep his hands off women. It's bad news either way. You have to judge a group not by its worst representatives but its best!"

"Look here," retorted Chris, "good or bad they're a menace. I want no part of them. If a guy wants to live that way that's his business but . . . ."

He was cut short in his answer by the appearance in the doorway of a hospital aide bringing in a tray of food. Presently both men were engrossed in putting a fork through a clump of overcooked broccoli and a piece of tired meat. By the half-warm temperature of the food before him Bill judged that their room must be at least two miles from the kitchen! He started to say, "If we can put a man on the moon why can't we . . . ." But he thought better of complaining and proceeded instead to chase some elusive Jello with a spoon that somehow seemed too small.

The meal over and the trays collected, it was Chris who chose to pursue the subject of the morning further. "I can't figure why a family guy like you should get so worked up about gays. I never went to college but I've got enough sense to know right from wrong."

Bill was prepared to continue. The noontime coffee, cool though it was, had perked him up. "Right before lunch, Chris, you said, 'If a guy *wants* to live that way that's his business.' People don't choose their sexual identity. They don't want to be male or female, they just are. One day you woke up and discovered that girls attracted you. Some guys wake up and discover that they aren't attracted to girls. The chemistry just isn't there. They find themselves drawn instead to male companionship. You may say that that isn't natural. But it's natural to them! The same holds for women who are attracted to other women. You didn't choose to be heterosexual. Most gays didn't choose to be homosexual."

Chris was softening some, but not so Bill could notice. "How'd you get so interested in homosexuals?" he asked.

"I got started on the subject in a big way from dealing with kids in school. I discovered how uninformed I was. I was 'street smart' but not 'book smart.' For example, I discovered that sex isn't a simple either/or. We are all a mix of male and female. Some people suffer pain, mostly from society, because their mix is different from that of the majority. They experience what some psychologists call a 'gender identity crisis.' They are male on the outside but female on the inside —or vice versa. In other words they are one thing physically and another thing psychically."

Chris became a bit defensive. He took it that Bill was trying to "one-up" him by dropping heavy terms that only shrinks and college types could understand. He felt overmatched but not defeated. "Look, I don't follow you all the way. When you start talking about an 'identity crisis' and use a word like 'psychically' you stop me. While you were off learning stuff like that, I was punching a time clock down at the plant trying to earn a decent living for the family. All the same, I still say I'm right. Where would the next generation come from if everyone was homosexual? D'ja ever think of that?"

Bill had had enough philosophy to remember how Immanuel Kant had suggested that human conduct should be tested by the principle of universality. If your behavior were multiplied the world over—what then? It surprised him that Chris had stumbled upon the same reasoning.

"Chris," he responded, "for a whole lot of reasons the human race has never been 100 percent reproductive. Sterility, impotence, sickness—you name it. Everyone doesn't have to reproduce in order for the race to survive. Only 5 percent of the population is homosexual. I wouldn't call that a threat to the future, would you?"

Chris was not in the mood to make any further concessions. In what might be described as a mildly defiant attitude he said, "I don't want to argue anymore. I only know what I feel inside. The whole homo package just isn't right!"

Bill wasn't one to pull rank, and it disturbed him that Chris felt bullied. In his friendliest voice he responded, "I don't like to argue. It's not my nature. And I am not trying to convert you to my way of thinking. It's just that I think some very serious injustices have been done by society in general to men and women—those five in every hundred—who discovered one day that they were different from the rest of us."

Bill would have continued in this conciliatory tone had not Chris's wife come in bearing a neatly wrapped package of fruit and cookies. She soon met her husband's friend from the city. In a matter of minutes, through shared food and conversation, Room 738 came to resemble, in spirit, a living room at home.

That mood was to prevail throughout the evening. At ten that night Chris angled his rented television set so that Bill could join him in watching the evening news. Both men were one in the world that they experienced but different in how they experienced it.

The early hours of the following day were spent on matters that are routine in hospitals. Doctors stopped in. Temperatures were taken. Uniformed aides filled water pitchers. Volunteers wheeled in a cart of books and sundries. An enterprising youngster came through hustling the morning paper.

When the room regained its rightful calm, Bill and Chris could be found leafing through the day's news. Bill was homesick for *The New York Times* but knew that it was not fair to judge a small-town paper by so lofty a standard. As his eyes skated over a hard-hitting editorial on the need to be sure that all the lights were out in the county court house overnight, Bill caught sight of a third person who had entered the room.

He was a man in his middle years—trim and nicely gray around the temples. Behind his rimless mountings, friendly eyes looked out.

Clad in a spotlessly clean doctor's type jacket, the man drew near. The name tag over the breast pocket solved the mystery—the man was Chaplain Carter.

The orthopedic floor is generally an easy floor for chaplains. Seldom the pathos there that one is likely to find where heart patients or victims of cancer gather. Knowing this, Chaplain Carter always finished up his morning rounds visiting patients who had nothing more seriously wrong with them than a broken bone or two. He gave his prime time, earlier in the day, to those who were likely to need something more than a passing word of cheer.

Having met the chaplain on previous visits, Chris made the necessary introduction. Before long it was clear that the room was a microcosm of ecumenism. The chaplain confessed to being a Methodist. Chris acknowleged (something the chaplain already knew) that he was a "World Series" Lutheran—in church only on the big days—Christmas Eve, Palm Sunday, and Easter. Bill laid claim to being an Episcopalian who had shelved his faith during college years but returned to it after the children came.

"Pastor Carter," said Chris, after things had quieted down, "Bill here and I got into a discussion yesterday on whether it's OK for a guy to be a homo. While I admit that I don't wear out the church, I remember enough about the Bible to know that that sorta thing is wrong. Right?"

The chaplain found himself wishing he were elsewhere, but he braved a smile, leaned forward in his chair, and attempted a response.

"It's true, Chris, that the Old Testament frowns on homosexuality. The prohibitions are rather clear and strict. But we have to remember that the Hebrews were a hard-pressed minority in those years and understandably concerned that their future be insured. They didn't want the 'chosen people' to die out. Homosexualty was a 'no no' largely on practical grounds. At least that's how I see it.

"Jesus never spoke to the subject, as far as we know. Paul wrote strongly against it, but we should keep in mind that his thoughts on such matters were highly influenced by Jewish training and conditioning. Besides, he lacked our psychological insights on the subject."

Chris was visibly disappointed that the chaplain had not come down hard with both feet on his side. The wedding band on the appropriate finger of the chaplain's left hand kept the burly patient from going any further with the thought that Carter might be gay himself.

Not wishing to leave the matter hanging on mere negative assertions, the chaplain went on: "It is clear to me that for those of us who claim to be Christians, all that the Bible says must submit to the mind of Jesus. He is Lord of the scriptures as well as Lord of the sabbath. The mind of Christ—that's what our religion is all about.

"And while it is true that Jesus has been enlisted over the years to support a variety of questionable views and causes, it is still true, and clearly so to me, that love is what mattered most with him, and ultimately *all* that mattered. Love is the final test. The point of life is love."

"You mean," chipped in Bill, "that we must deal with everyone, homosexuals included, out of love and not out of a desire to exclude or punish?"

"Exactly," said the chaplain. "For too long a time now we have made life difficult for homosexuals. We have made them the butt of cruel jokes and epithets, treated them like criminals, made them feel unwelcome in our clubs and churches, driven them to such a point of desperation that they have had to go against their generally sensitive nature and become militant in order to gain the basic rights that belong to them as human beings. They didn't closet themselves. It was we who drove them into hiding!"

Chris wasn't buying the chaplain's case. With a series of quick movements—as if to demonstrate his masculinity—he lit up a cigarette and sought to bring the conversation down to earth.

"Let me ask you one question, Pastor. If two gays came up to you and asked you to marry them to each other would you do it?" Thinking that he had reduced the chaplain's position to absurdity he was taken by surprise when Carter answered slowly, "Not exactly."

Rising from a chair the chaplain strolled toward the window and went on: "By my understanding of marriage I couldn't marry two consenting homosexuals to each other. Even if the law permitted it —which it doesn't—I couldn't. But if I were sure that two homosexual adults really loved each other and were willing to commit themselves to a relationship that included intended permanence, I would not hesitate to solemnize their vows.

Overheard in Room 738

"Getting back to Jesus—if love is the cardinal virtue, and two people truly love each other, why should they be denied the right to openly express that love because their sexuality is different?"

"I can't believe what I'm hearing," Chris shouted. "You'd actually say a prayer over two gays who wanted to set up house? How long do you think it would last?"

"How long did your first marriage last, Chris?" the chaplain asked as kindly as he could. The color rushed to Chris's cheeks and rendered him silent.

"Forgive me for getting personal, Chris. I merely wanted to show that we all come short of our best intentions."

"Do you think homosexual activity should be punishable by law?" Bill asked. "What do you think?" returned the chaplain.

Bill said, "No, I really don't. Where consenting adults are involved, I don't see that it's a matter for the police or courts. However, I think people—especially youngsters—ought to be protected by law against those who force themselves sexually on others. That goes for gays and straights alike."

"Of course," said the chaplain. "I think everyone would agree on that."

With that word a genial attendant moved in to set up shop for lunch. When the trays were in place and the covers removed from the dishes, the chaplain, standing between the beds in 738, smiled and said, "It looks as if that food might have been blessed before. But let's bless it again anyway."

He offered up a simple prayer of thanks and left.

February 17, 1974

The Case for Reparations

On Sunday morning, May 4, 1969, Mr. James Foreman, representing the National Black Economic Development Conference, disrupted the Riverside morning worship service and issued a "Black Manifesto" to the Christian churches of the land in general and The Riverside Church in particular. On July 13, 1969, Dr. Campbell responded to Mr. Foreman with this sermon.

> *And if I have defrauded any one*
> *of anything, I restore it fourfold.*
> *—Luke 19:8*

THERE ARE SAFER and more manageable subjects for a lazy Sunday in midsummer than the one we have singled out today, "The Case for Reparations." But there is a tide in the affairs of men that is no respecter of preferences. Some themes choose us, we do not choose them.

One thing I need not do today is win you to an affection for

Zacchaeus. You already like this friend of Jesus. Most everyone does. Handicapped by a lack of height, he draws us out. With a name like Zacchaeus he probably sat in the back row in school and missed a lot of what went on up front. But chiefly we warm to Zacchaeus because in his zeal to see the Man from Nazareth he was willing to abandon his dignity by running down the street and climbing a tree.

Jesus rewarded Zacchaeus' zeal by stopping before that tree and bidding the publican come down. "Zacchaeus," said Jesus, "make haste and come down; for I must stay at your house today."

It must have been a walk to end all walks, that walk of Jesus and Zacchaeus to the publican's house. If only we could have bugged *that* conversation. Zacchaeus was a tax collector. His job was to raise money from his own people on behalf of the occupying country, hated Rome. As I understand it, it was a cost-plus operation. He paid so much for the franchise and all that he made beyond that price was his. It was a case of "all the traffic can bear." Apparently Zacchaeus saw to it that the traffic bore plenty.

But now it's different: Zacchaeus sees his job in a new light. He sees other people as he had not seen them before. He sees money in what for him is a startlingly fresh perspective. Listen to him now! "Behold, Lord, the half of my goods I give to the poor; and if I have defrauded any one of anything, I restore it fourfold." Walking with Jesus will do that to a person.

More important than this remarkable resolution of Zacchaeus is the response of Jesus. He pronounces words of unqualified approval. He gives it his blessing. He speaks the reassuring "Amen." For Jesus said to him, "Today salvation has come to this house, since he also is a son of Abraham."

There were two elements in the reclamation of Zacchaeus: *Generosity* ("Half of my goods I give to the poor"), and *Justice* ("If I have defrauded any one of anything, I restore it fourfold"). To put it differently, Zacchaeus made reparation. Let's not fear the term. The principle is as old as the book of Exodus, and as new as contemporary jurisprudence. In the twenty-second chapter of Exodus we read, "If a man steals an ox or a sheep, and kills it or sells it, he shall pay five oxen for an ox, and four sheep for a sheep. He shall make restitution." Roman law insisted that a man who stole had to repay fourfold. Zacchaeus goes beyond Roman law by suggesting that he will make amends for *any* injustice that he may have been responsible for.

The principle has a place in Jewish theology. I quote from the *Standard Jewish Encyclopedia:* "Forgiveness of sin depends upon true repentance while a wrong done to a fellow-man requires rectification and restitution before forgiveness is possible." Roman Catholic Moral Theology puts it this way. "Restitution is an act of commutative justice whereby property is restored to one who has been deprived of it by unjust damage or threat."

It wasn't so long ago that a very reputable, conservative, orthodox, Baptist theologian, A. H. Strong, writing on repentance, said: "True repentance is indeed manifested and evidenced by confession of sin before God and by *reparation* for wrongs done to men." It was out of such considerations that the World Council of Churches in its first consultation ever on racism, held in London this May, endorsed the principle of reparation. Forgiveness without reparation becomes an indulgence in cheap grace. "Behold, Lord, . . . if I have defrauded any one of anything, I restore it fourfold."

It is against this background that our response to the Black Manifesto should be made. Surely it is beyond dispute by now that white people in this country have not done right by the Blacks. Before a Black child says his first word or takes his first step in our society he is handicapped. The discrimination we work is *sometimes personal* and *always systemic.* That system dates back to slavery, which was instituted by our forebears, but it has been perpetuated and confirmed by us, their children, to our political, material, and social advantage.

Wherein have we sinned, you ask?

We have sinned as educators by failing to give Americans, Black and white, a knowledge of the history of this country's largest minority group.

We have sinned as jurists by finding one loophole after another with which to strangle the Black person's hope for justice.

We have sinned as parents by passing on to our children the myth of white supremacy, and enforcing it by innuendo, poor example and sick humor.

We have sinned as tourists by coming up against "white only" signs in restaurants, hotels, swimming pools, and theaters without so much as a word of protest.

We have sinned as sports fans by cheering the exploits of the Black athlete and caring little for the athlete's welfare as a person.

The Case for Reparations

We have sinned as bankers by restricting the flow of capital into the Black community.

We have sinned as trade unionists by denying apprentice status to Blacks and failing to welcome them as fellow-workers.

We have sinned as members of clubs, fraternities and lodges by restricting membership to people like ourselves.

We have sinned as legislators by catering to racist pressures and encumbering the path to justice with laws designed to retard progress and make elementary right and wrong appear more complicated than they need to be.

We have sinned as members of the entertainment world by foisting on the American public an image of the Black as a shiftless, drawling, less than human thing.

And we have sinned as ministers of the gospel by stooping to deliver bland assurances that all was well, while the acids of racism were eating away the nation's soul and Jesus was being driven back to Golgatha!

Our greatest failure as a church lies in our unwillingness or inability, or both, to carry faith beyond the interpersonal level and make it operative at the social and corporate levels.

Martin Luther gave us a good steer when he said,

One who lives in a community must do his share in bearing and suffering the community's burdens, dangers, and injuries, even though, not he, but his neighbor has caused them: He must do this in the same way that he enjoys the peace, profit, protection, wealth, freedom and convenience of the community, even though he has not won them or brought them into being.

We have had the numbers and the power to make a difference, and we have not made that difference. Therein lies our guilt. They also sin who only stand and watch!

We have failed collectively as white Christians, and we can make amends collectively. This is what reparation means to me. Oh I know there are objections. I've been combing them out of my hair for the last two months. How can damage to a person's soul be repaid by money? It can't. What we have done to the Blacks in this country is beyond repayment in terms of dollars and cents. We untribed them, we unfamilied them, we depersonalized them.

I confess that I could not read without weeping that section in the *Autobiography of Malcolm X,* where he talks about going to

Chicago to get a new name to replace the one we had given him when his family was a chattel in the slave system. Listen to him:

My application had, of course, been made and during this time I received from Chicago my "X." The Muslim's "X" symbolized the true African family name that he never could know. For me, my "X" replaced the white slavemaster name of "Little" which some blue-eyed devil named Little had imposed upon my paternal forebears. The receipt of my "X" meant that forever after in the nation of Islam, I would be known as Malcolm X. Mr. Muhammad taught that we would keep this "X" until God Himself returned and gave us a Holy Name from His own mouth.

There is no money that can make up for this. But our money can be an earnest of a good intention, and can hint at a new direction for the church and for the nation.

"Why can't we call it something other than reparations, I don't like the term?" More is involved than a squabble over semantics. The term must be reckoned with not only because it is in the Manifesto but because once we get away from it we are going to do again what "Whitey" has done for hundreds of years, make a few gifts here and there and pride ourselves on our generosity. All such gifts have a way of flattering the donor and debasing the recipient. *That which we are called upon to do does not come under the category of generosity. It belongs to justice.* The term reparation insures that insight. The good Samaritan was generous. He only *found* his victim in the ditch, we *put* ours there.

"But others have claims—the American Indian, the Spanish American, the Eskimo, the deprived people of Appalachia. Where does the whole thing end?" One claim does not cancel out another. What sort of logic is this? *Each case* deserves its day in court before the conscience of the church and nation.

"Isn't it morbid to talk about guilt? Isn't it depressing? Doesn't it have a backward look and make impossible that forward looking stance so sorely needed?"

Most people who feel this way have a habit of coupling the word "guilt" with prejudicial qualifiers. They talk about "morbid" guilt or "fruitless" introspection. As any minister or priest knows full well, guilt *can become* pathological. One can become excessively preoccupied with it. But this need not be so. I am not suggesting that guilt should be the only component of our response to the Black people. I insist that it is a component. True repentance has a way of not only looking back, but of motivating us for the work that waits our doing.

"What difference would it make if this church and every other church got with it?" Not much. There isn't all that much wealth even with old and new money combined. But the church could very well be used of God as a catalytic agent to loosen sizable sums from other sectors of American life, notably business and government.

"Why should we help the Black people? My parents were foreign born. They came over and made good without any outside help?" The answer is that the cases are not similar. Your parents came voluntarily. These people were brought over under our compulsion. Moreover, by the accident of color they were denied assimilation into normal American life—a deprivation European immigrants did not face.

The most serious objection of all, however, is this: "Why should I support a revolution?" My answer is "You shouldn't. And you don't have to!" One of the most distinguished theologians in American Protestantism confided in me privately how regretful he was that we do not have a better document as a symbol of the current confrontation. He was referring to the fact that the Black Manifesto has a sad way of confusing two issues—reparations and revolution. Revolution is always a possibility. We went that route ourselves vis-à-vis England. Doubtless there will always be some in any political state who are convinced that revolution is called for. They will act accordingly. *But it is madness to expect people who do not share that conviction to contribute to it.* Suicide no less than racism is a sin.

Tragically the Black Manifesto puts two loyalties on a collision course—a belated loyalty to the Black people in their quest for justice, and a loyalty to country. It is a recognized parliamentary procedure that a member who requests it may have a question divided. I ask, therefore, that this question be divided. Reparations? Yes! Revolution? No! As clearly as I can I want to say that no funds that I give, no funds that I raise, no funds over which I have an influence will be used for the destruction or overthrow of this government. I believe we need reform. I believe we stand in need of drastic overhaul and renewal from the inside out. But I don't believe God is finished yet with this republic!

If the revolutionary talk in the Manifesto, the Marxist line that marks its opening pages, were only an attention-getting device, it has served its purpose and ought to be honorably retired, so that we can get on with the business of making reparations that lead not to revolution, but to reconciliation. "God was in Christ reconciling the world to himself, . . . *and entrusting to us the message of reconciliation.*" This is our ultimate commitment as Christians.

Let me change the figure and introduce at the same time a touching bit of dialogue from John Steinbeck's play, *The Short Reign of Pippin IV.* The king in disguise comes to the little French town of Gambais where he notices, as he nears a castle, that a bust of Pan has been removed from its pedestal and thrown into the moat. Pippin asks an old man "How did he get in the moat?" "Oh someone pushed him in. They always do, sometimes two or three times a year." "But why?" "Who knows?" said the old man. "There's people that push things in the moat. Pretty hard work too. There's just people that push things in the moat."

A little later the king asks gently, "Are you the owner here?" "No," he said, "I'm not. I live hereabouts." "Then why do you pull them out?" The old man looked puzzled and searched for an answer. "Why—I don't know. I guess there's people that pull things out— that's what they do. . . . I guess that's how things get done." People that push things in and people that pull things out—we have a choice.

Rather than begrudge reparations I should think that we would rejoice that our sin in part is reparationable. How that drunk hit-and-run driver who killed a little girl last night wishes he could make reparation! We still have time, and history has remained sufficiently set to allow us this response.

I am not presumptuous enough to suggest that this is *the Christian* response to reparation. I am simply saying that it is *this Christian's* response. "And Zacchaeus stood and said to the Lord, 'If I have defrauded any one of anything, I restore it fourfold.'" What do *you* make of *that?*

July 13, 1969

An Open Letter to Billy Graham

A Preliminary Statement

COME NEXT JUNE I will have been in the ministry twenty-five years. Never in all that time did I use the format that I plan to use today—the open letter.

The concerns that prompted an open letter to Billy Graham will become apparent as I read it. I address myself, not so much to Billy Graham the man, as to the position he represents in the religious life of America. The aim is to generate national discussion on the issues raised.

The President's announcement last night that bombing in North Vietnam north of the 20th parallel will soon be suspended does not materially affect the argument of this letter—although the letter was completed and released prior to that announcement.

Dr. Graham was apprised last Friday by telegram that this open letter would be read today. A copy of the full text was airmailed to him that same day.

An Open Letter to Billy Graham

Dear Dr. Graham:

Greetings in the name of our Lord and Savior Jesus Christ. I address you as a fellow-minister of the gospel and as one who has more respect for the work you represent than you might at first suspect. My earlier years were spent in the theological tradition in which you make your home. In search of an education both of us touched down at the same college—although at different times. We met once, more than twenty years ago, in the Pocono Mountains of Pennsylvania, and share a host of mutual friends, including your able chorister Cliff Barrows.

Knowing from some modest experience in the field the severe strains and pressures that go with itinerant preaching, I commend you for your remarkable durability and fiscal integrity. You have worn with meekness the honors and recognition that have come your way. Your zeal and commitment are as strong today as when you started. I have long envied your composure under fire and your ability to parry skillfully with reporters in neutral or hostile settings.

The immediate provocation for this open letter is your failure, to date, to respond to a telegram sent to you at your Montreat, North Carolina address on December 20, 1972 by the Rev. Dr. Henry W. Andersen, in his capacity as chairman for Key '73 in the Chicagoland area. Dr. Andersen is the respected pastor of the First Presbyterian Church of LaGrange, Illinois. He has graciously shared with me the full text of his telegram, part of which was reported in *The New York Times* on December 23. The entire message read:

Dear Dr. Graham:

I have sent telegrams to President Nixon deploring the unlimited bombing the United States is unleashing on Vietnam.

My voice before the President is nothing, but you have access to him that no other minister of God has. If you deplore the bombing also, I beg you to raise your voice as a prophet, like Nathan of old, in protest to the President, imploring him to stop the bombing immediately.

Bombing any time is despicable—but to renew unlimited bombing when "peace is at hand," and to beat the Vietnamese to their knees, and to kill thousands more in the name of peace, just so that we can have our way, *is outrageous.*

In the name of the Prince of Peace, Jesus Christ, our Lord and Savior, do something to stop it!

/s/ Dr. Henry W. Andersen
Chicagoland and Key '73 Chairman

An Open Letter to Billy Graham

Your long-standing friendship with Richard Nixon is well known, as is your public endorsement of his candidacy for reelection to the office of President. There is nothing amiss here. The President is entitled to supportive friends. Every citizen has a right to back the nominee of his or her choice.

Dr. Andersen's unanswered telegram, however, stresses the stewardship of privilege. As scripture puts it, "To whom much is given, of him will much be required." Most of us in this country, whether clerical or lay, are like many of our modern highways: we are "limited access" people. Under the providence of God you have been afforded generous access to the inner circles that develop and execute national policy. As one of the "near voices" within hearing distance of the throne you surely bear a responsibility to critique government policy as well as bless it. The President needs a Micaiah not a Zedekiah, a prophet, not a mere house chaplain.

What are we to conclude from your silence in the face of Dr. Andersen's request? Those of us who pastor local congregations know with what heaviness of heart our people celebrated Christmas this year. How could it be otherwise when, by presidential command, bombing missions were resumed over North Vietnam when peace negotiations hit a snag in Paris? Christmas bells and B-52 bombing raids are a hard mix to assimilate.

What are we to conclude from your silence? At least five possibilities suggest themselves:

1. *You did not receive the message.* Should this be the case there is still time to respond.

2. *You received the message and made some unreported effort to influence the President to stop the bombing.* Should this be the case it is crucially important to the integrity of religion in this country that you make your efforts known. Since your areas of agreement with the present administration are widely known, your areas of disagreement should be duly publicized in the interest of giving the American people an accurate picture of your relationship to presidential power.

3. *You received the message and did not agree with its agonizing appraisal of the bombing.* In this case we would hope that you would share your reasoning with us to the relief of our tortured and indig-

nant souls. If you have a justifying word, you owe it to your suffering compatriots to speak it.

4. *You received the message and agree with its general intent but fear that any forthright declaration you might make would jeopardize your connections with the Establishment.* In this case we would respectfully suggest that your "in" with the powers that be is being sustained at too high a price. At what point does friendship with the world amount to enmity with God?

5. *You received the message, sympathized with its basic sentiment, but lacked a theological rationale for speaking out.* In this case we would hope that you would rediscover the richness and boldness of the prophetic tradition recorded in the scriptures. Evangelists across the years have been known for their ability to come down hard on personal sins, and for their inability (with a few notable exceptions) to address themselves to matters of public morality and the common good. There is no sound reason, theological or otherwise, why this should be so. Selective silence damages the cause of Christ.

The telegram in question was sent by a responsible brother in Christ on behalf of a responsible body of church men and women who believe deeply in evangelism. Moreover, those who dispatched that message are representative of thousands across the country who are questing for a form of evangelism that has for its aim something more than the interior rejuvenation of individual men and women. They want an evangelism that touches all of life.

So much for the immediate provocation that prompted this open correspondence. Let me move on and speak to a related concern that rises from a deeper provocation of many years' standing. That concern has to do with the essential nature of biblical religion.

It appears to me that Christians in this country, regardless of denomination or tradition, are becoming increasingly divided into two camps. On the one hand are those who see the religious life as centering in a personal experience of God that finds expression in acts of private and corporate devotion and individual deeds of kindness. On the other hand are those who see the religious life as going beyond the personal to include responsible corporate action at those points in society where justice has been thwarted.

The question at issue here is what we make of history. Those who interpret the new life in Christ in strictly personal terms are saying, in effect, that history has no value in itself and is useful only insofar as it provides occasions for the soul to be found of God. In this view, history is a disposable wrapper that could hardly matter less. Such matters as economic injustices, racial discrimination, unemployment, war, housing for the poor, questionable national priorities, are not legitimate concerns of faith. Salvation does not catapult human beings into history, it helps them to endure history until they enter upon the larger life above.

Whether you intend it so or not, sir, this in broad strokes is what your position looks like to outsiders like myself. If this is an unfair characterization of your position I would welcome your corrections. If this is a fair and reasonable impression of where you stand, I should like to raise with you the following questions:

1. The Holy Spirit who indwells believers is the same Spirit that brought creation into being. How can anything in the created order (e.g. history) be "off limits" to those who have the Spirit in their hearts?

2. History may be transient and ambiguous, but biblical religion takes history seriously. God is the Lord of history. Christ came into history. Christians have from the beginning prayed that God's will may be done *on earth,* even as it is in heaven. At the end of time we look for a new heaven *and a new earth.* Some of the church's finest hours have come when believers bent to the task of grappling with entrenched evil against long odds. How can one disparage history and be continuous with biblical revelation?

3. Those who disavow social action as a proper expression of Christian faith become the willing or unwilling advocates of the status quo. What does this say to minority groups and other oppressed peoples for whom the status quo is a source of pain and deprivation?

4. *Christianity Today* in its issue of December 22, 1972, quotes you as saying that President Nixon will "be putting a lot more emphasis on moral and spiritual affairs" in his second term because he realizes that "the greatest problem we're facing is moral permissiveness and decadence." Does the term "moral" have to do with matters of personal rectitude alone or does it have to do as well with the making of war, the spending of public moneys, the flow of justice in

the courts, the abolition of racial discrimination, the availability of adequate housing to every citizen, tax reform, and other issues that affect the structures under which we live together as a people?

5. In representing the life of faith as a personal transaction with God what does one make of the social pronouncements of the prophets, Mary's Magnificat, the quotation from Isaiah with which Jesus inaugurated his ministry in the synagogue at Nazareth, and the vision of the final judgment in Matthew 25 where the question of "knowing Christ" is decided on the basis of one's identification with the hungry, the thirsty, the naked, the sick, and the imprisoned?

Because of your high visibility you have a unique opportunity to give dramatic definition to a form of evangelism that is equally comfortable confronting men and women with the claims of the gospel or calling the nation to a new fidelity to social righteousness. Migrant workers, welfare families, prisoners, ghetto school children, American Indians and many others would be heartened by your advocacy. Given the kind of world we have today, withheld advocacy on the part of Christians gives substance to the charge that our faith is irrelevant.

The gospel needs to be articulated in our society. But it can also be argued that the gospel needs very much to become incarnate in our society in the form of persons who are willing to use their power on behalf of the powerless. The Word made flesh should not be made mere word again.

The two camps earlier alluded to are real, but they need not be accepted as representing altogether fixed positions. Indeed, one of the heartening signs on the horizon is the motion that one senses on both sides. Evangelicals here and there are warming to works inspired by a troubled social conscience, while many who have majored in the reformation of society are rediscovering the importance of personal trust in God.

Key '73 represents a glittering opportunity for Christians in this country to come to terms with the comprehensiveness of the gospel. It could well provide the occasion for the closing of ranks and the beginning of a rousing effort to call this nation to unprecedented heights of faith and obedience. A new conception of evangelism is struggling to be born. You can help to hasten its appearance.

With this letter comes an invitation to preach in The Riverside

Church in response to these issues and questions. We will arrange a format that will make provision for discussion and exchange. All that is needed is your consent and a mutually convenient time.

I know that you will receive this communication in the spirit in which it is sent—the spirit of openness and genuine concern.

The stakes are high. The time is short. The nation is badly torn. Is there no balm in Gilead? Why then is the health of our people not recovered?

Sincerely,
Ernest T. Campbell

December 31, 1972

Editor's Note: Billy Graham did not respond to Dr. Campbell's Open Letter. However, in a statement to the press several weeks following the sermon, Dr. Graham described himself as a New Testament evangelist rather than an Old Testament prophet.

Adam's Other Son

> *And Adam knew his wife again, and she bore a son and called his name Seth.*
>
> —*Genesis 4:25*

MY SUBJECT TODAY is "Adam's Other Son." That title sounds like a clue for a crossword puzzle. The offspring of Adam and Eve . . . Let's see . . . four letters . . . Cain . . . That won't do. It must begin with an A. Abel—of course . . . No. That won't fit. The name must end in h . . . Adam's other son . . . whoever could it. be?

The word "other" suggests a person that we have a way of overlooking—the one who gets away from us; someone whose identity we have not troubled ourselves to learn. Adam and Eve we know. Cain and Abel we know. But it's a good bet that not one person in ten on the next No. 5 bus going north would be able to give Seth as the name of Adam's other son! "And Adam knew his wife," says the record, "and she bore a son and called his name Seth."

Seth. I've met but one person in my life thus far who bore that name. I'm aware of a clock that bears that name, and that's about it, I'm afraid. *But it is my belief that the obscurity of Seth can be instructive.*

Adam's Other Son

Seth's obscurity illustrates the world's tendency to notice the very good and the very bad and ignore the ordinary individual. Anyone who knows the Bible at all knows Cain. In our age of violence and anti-heroes we are actually drawn to Cain. There is a sense in which we find him fascinating. He was not slow about expressing himself, his brother's blood can testify to that. He was marked by God for his own protection—an early sign of grace. Writers over the years have let their imagination play with that mark of Cain. The term has become a byword in the language. He was made to be a nomad and a fugitive, and it isn't hard to romanticize that—especially for a generation that has lots of Gypsy blood running in its veins.

The truth is that evil attracts us. Blake spoke for many in our time when he observed that "active evil is better than passive good."

All the same, Cain, by any measurement, was a wicked man. He is the first murderer on record. He slew his brother, and not, we may suppose, for any lack in his environment. His heart was evil.

I was interested in a comment that one of our state senators, John Marchi, made a while ago when speaking about the relationship of crime to environment: "Poverty is hardly an all-encompassing explanation for violent crime. Why did Cain slay Abel? Was it because there weren't enough figs on the trees?" Hardly.

Had the mass media been alive in the days of Cain, he surely would have made the 10:00 o'clock news and probably rated a headline in some morning tabloid. Anyone who knows the Bible knows Cain.

And just about anyone who knows the Bible knows Abel: the victim, the patron saint of all who have been treacherously done in. He was a good man. So good in fact that his righteousness incited the jealousy and anger of his brother. The record says that, "The Lord had regard for Abel and his offering, but for Cain and his offering he had no regard." Some people have seized upon that comment to talk about the importance of blood sacrifice. Others have said that it illustrates the tension between the nomad with his animals, and the farmer and his crops. I think it is not so complicated. The *offerer,* Abel, was of superior righteousness to the *offerer,* Cain, who conceived wickedness in his heart. This comes out later when God says to Cain, "If you do well, will you not be accepted?"

Abel stands out in the minds of people as a person of relative innocence and exceptional goodness—so good, in fact, as to incite the envy of his brother. Anyone who knows the Bible knows Abel.

But who remembers Seth? He's the other one, the one who turned out all right. He is the ordinary one, in the literal meaning of that term, "of the usual order." Nothing more is said of him than this: "To Seth also a son was born, and he called his name Enosh." That was his only known accomplishment.

Yet, to his parents, he awakened hope. Eve remembered the promise about the seed of the woman bruising the serpent's head. With Abel dead and Cain a fugitive how would this promise be fulfilled? In a word, its future lay with Seth.

"And Adam knew his wife again, and she bore a son and called his name Seth."

Seth's obscurity is a reminder of our own obscurity. When you read a story out of the past you have a way of saying to yourself, "Well, if I were in that story, I would be this one, or that one." In this story I can see myself only as Seth. Yes, I have known anger, but never to the point of murder. I have had flashes of goodness (not too-long sustained at any given time), but I have never been so devout or so obedient or so exceptionally committed as to arouse the jealousy of someone else. In short, I am, if I am like anyone in the story, most like Seth.

There is a striving after greatness that gives expression to legitimate ambition. But there is also a striving after greatness that represents an insane passion for what we cannot be. Let's face it. Most of us are destined to be the children of Seth. There are probably ten thousand singers in the five boroughs. How many are really known? Does that mean that if we sing and are not known, we should go to bed every night tossing with envy, jealousy, and discontentment? There are thousands of people in the United States who teach philosophy to eager students. But the philosophers who are widely known in our time you could count on the fingers of one hand. What then of the others? Are they to sulk in resented obscurity?

Only a few economists are invited to Washington to put on their glasses and tell us what's coming up. Does this mean that all others who study those nasty figures should go around feeling sorry for themselves? Hundreds and hundreds of actors and actresses abound in these United States. Most people, if you stopped them cold, could name no more than half a dozen. There are multiplied tens of thousands of nurses working earnestly in our time, but ask someone to name a nurse and she would probably say Florence Nightingale!

To compensate for our obscurity we like to lay on our titles, whip up our public relations, fancy up our stationery, and talk up our achievements. May I be personal and say that I've long since given up trying to be a better preacher than Dr. This or Dr. That, or Dr. Other. What I'm really trying to do is be a better preacher than I was last week.

Seth comes upon the scene, marries, sires, and dies. And that's about the way it is with us so far as worldly note is concerned. When we die most of us will be listed without comment. The question is whether this fact, indisputable and largely unchangeable, is to make us perpetually discontented with our lot. To put it more positively, what I'm hoping for is that more of us will come to trust our own sample of life. We are led to believe, by advertising especially, that real living is going on somewhere else. It really isn't, you know. Trust your sample of life.

Years ago I heard the story of a man who came back very happy from a vacation. A friend stopped him and asked him where he'd been. He said, "I've just had two great weeks in Atlantic City." Later in the day another acquaintance came up and said, "Where have you been? We missed you Harry." Harry replied, "I've been in Atlantic City and I had a great time." "Did you have dinner at Charlie's Fish House?" the friend asked. Harry said, "No." "Harry," said the friend, "everyone who goes to Atlantic City goes there." Harry bumped into still another friend who said, "Atlantic City, Harry, did you get to go to one of those showroom auctions on the boardwalk?" Harry said, "No." The friend said, "Listen, when you go to Atlantic City, you should never miss the auction." You guessed it, a fourth friend approached him: "We've missed you, Harry, where have you been?" Harry said, "Atlantic City." The friend said, "Did you ride a bike on the boardwalk early in the morning?" Harry said he hadn't. The friend said, "How can you go to Atlantic City and not rent a bike?" Toward the end of the day he met one last friend, who said, "Harry, we've missed you. Where have you been?" Harry said, "I ain't been nowhere, and I ain't seen nuthin!" Within our terms, Harry didn't have the guts to trust his own sample of life.

The best parts of human history are never written at all: family life, patient service, quiet endurance, the training of children, resistance to evil. Shakespeare knew this so well:

When in disgrace with fortune and men's eyes
I all alone beweep my outcast state,
And trouble deaf heaven with my bootless cries,
And look upon myself, and curse my fate;
Wishing me like to one more rich in hope,
Featur'd like him, like him with friends
    possess'd,
Desiring this man's art, and that man's scope,
With what I most enjoy contented least;
Yet in these thoughts myself almost despising,
Haply I think on thee—and then my state,
Like to the lark at break of day arising
From sullen earth—sings hymns at heaven's gate;
For thy sweet love remember'd such wealth brings
That then I scorn to change my state with kings.

—Sonnet XXIX

"And Adam knew his wife again, and she bore a son and called his name Seth."

Finally, *Seth's obscurity is a reminder of the importance of ordinary people in the plan of God.* You see, Seth provided the continuity. As a youngster, believe it or not, I had to memorize the names of those who carried what some would call the "church line" from Adam right on down: Adam, Seth, Enosh, Kenan, Mahalalel, Jared, Lamech, etc. —all the way through Noah down to Abraham. It seemed like a waste of time. But in that line Seth is a link. He was a carrier of the promise, without whom the covenant, humanly speaking, would have gone spark out. After the homicide, God started again with Seth. He always does.

There is a strange perversity with God. He chooses the unspectacular Seth. He chooses an assortment of nomadic tribes to be his servant people. Every prophet in the Old Testament was an unlikely choice. He chooses a stable over a palace for his Son; a cross over a throne for the earthly climax of his ministry. And, as for the church —well, a glimpse of its earliest records will show that not many wise, not many powerful, not many of noble birth were called.

Adam's Other Son

We still prefer the star system. This may be one of our problems in this Bicentennial year. As various television programs take us back into the past, and we see recreated before our eyes illustrious people of compelling leadership, we ask ourselves, "Where are such saviors now?" For, speaking frankly, when one scans the political spectrum these days, one is hardly inspired to sing the Doxology. *Maybe God has given this age to Seth.* Maybe God is withholding the star from us, some human savior, to make us go into ourselves and develop our own capacities.

How many university presidents can you name today? How many corporation heads? How many preachers? It used to be, even within this century, that one could tick off a whole host of names in those fields. Americans instinctively look to the illustrious leader for deliverance. But there are no stars to speak of. This is the age of Seth. God has committed the ordering of life to ordinary people.

Consider this truth in connection with two critically important institutions. One is the home. Back in the twelfth century, a monk by the name of Benedict made a point that parents, actual or to-be, would be well advised to note: "Love thy children with impartial love; the hope oft errs that you place on the more promising, and all your joy may come from him that you have kept in the background."

The household is the most widespread economic community in the world. If all of the households of America looked to the ordering of their household, the change would be phenomenal! If all the Seths and their wives and children looked to their own values, and supported one another in love, we would have a new America. Someone put it this way, speaking of the home: "Nothing never happens." Something is always happening in the home, for good or for ill.

The other institution is the church. I know how small it looks. It hardly ever hits the papers. We are in a position today where we are neither refuted nor reported, just ignored. Yet, *the church is still the largest voluntary association in the world.* You're never too rich to belong; you're never too poor. You're never too young to belong; you're never too old. The church welcomes you in every stage of life.

I have a feeling that within the church today responsibility rests largely with Seth. We gave Dr. Jones a tough baptism of fire today with that New Testament lesson: Romans 16:3–16. If you think not, go home and try it yourself this afternoon. Who are these people?

Andronicus, Ampliatus, Urbanus, Stachys, Apelles, Herodion, Try-
phaena, Philologus, etc. (You don't even know whether I'm pro-
nouncing them correctly yourself!) Such folks comprised the church
in Paul's day. They were all Seths, every one of them! Most of them
were not even mentioned in a letter. The overwhelming majority
stayed anonymous. Sometime, not during the sermon, look through
the hymnbook and note the hymns that are marked "Anonymous":
"O Come, All Ye Faithful," "The First Noel," "Jesus, the Very
Thought of Thee," "Fairest Lord Jesus," "Jesus, Thou Joy of Loving
Hearts." Seth wrote them all!

As we install the officers of The Riverside Church today, we are
not to look upon them, or the ministers who install them, as in any
way stars or saviors. We are, all of us together, like Seth—seeking
collectively to understand the will of our Lord. "And Adam knew his
wife again, and she bore a son and called his name Seth." God must
love the Seths of the world, He made so many of us.

Who is Seth?

Seth is the one who is always there but seldom noticed.

His views on life are never sought.

He will *read* the news but never *make* the news.

He pays his bills on time and stays out of trouble with the law.

His life passes like the most regular of verbs:

> Punctually at work 5 days a week;
> Reliably at home each evening, save for the night he bowls;
> Keenly interested in his children and unfashionably loyal to
> his wife.

Seth is the neighbor upstairs who minds his business, but whose
smile is always friendly.

He is the man in the next pew who can count on one hand the
Sundays that he's missed.

He is seldom swept by a politician, but he always votes.

He cannot articulate his disgust with pornography, but he knows
that those who defend it in the name of art are wrong.

Seth seldom rides a cab.

He does not understand "capital gains" or "selling short," but
he makes a deposit every payday at a savings bank.

He would be lost in a gourmet restaurant, but he and the Mrs.

and the kids can get excited about a meal together at Howard Johnson's or a fried chicken picnic in the park.

His clothes are undistinguished and his travels few, but when the
hat is passed in the office for a sick friend, he always has a ten to spare.

Who is Seth?

Seth is the almost anonymous one.
His demands on life are modest,
   but his joys run deep.
He and his like are the stuff on which the order of a nation rests.
When he passes from the scene, few will notice.
But when he enters on the other side, it will be to the sound of
   trumpets,
And the singing of the heavenly hosts—for of such is the kingdom
   of God!

January 25, 1976

William Sloane Coffin Jr.

Senior Minister of The Riverside Church

1977–

Finally, you preach for yourself but, if you go down deep enough, you touch enough common humanity so that everyone's involved.
—William Sloane Coffin Jr.

The Spirit and the Power

This is the first sermon that Dr. Coffin preached as senior minister of The Riverside Church.

"For God did not give us a spirit of timidity but a spirit of power and love [2 Timothy 1:7]*."*

AT THIS POINT in the service I imagine a few personal words are in order. So to all members of Riverside Church let me say that I am totally disposed to cherish, nurture, and love each and every one of you, in the sure hope that you will do the same for me—as so many of you have done already! Among the problems of the church, I see none that is insoluble. To bring relief to the far-flung misery of New York City is obviously more complicated. The human rights about which we speak so often do not exhaust the gospel, but they are an essential part of it. Therefore, complex as these city problems may be, we cannot throw in the towel until there is food for all, housing for all, work for all, education and decent medical help for all. And finally, in the pursuit of my new duties, I promise that I will try always to heed the advice of whoever it was who said, "Take yourself lightly, so that, like angels, you may fly."

The Spirit and the Power

Now let us return to our text—"for God did not give us a spirit of timidity," or "craven spirit" as some of the translations read, "but a spirit of power and love." And let us also turn to the none too gentle words of our Lord and Savior—"to every one who has will more be given, but from him who has not, even what he has will be taken away."

It is hard to believe that this parable is as cruel as it sounds. It is hard to believe that Jesus is actually saying what the world seems so intent on proving, that the big-time always wins and that small-fry always lose. Is Jesus really joining the already all too numerous citizens of almost every nation who are intent on attacking the vulnerable instead of the powerful? Or is he simply trying, once again, to break through our defenses in order to unearth something that most of us would much prefer to keep buried?

My own conclusion is that this parable is harsh, but also strangely hopeful. New Yorkers live in an enormous city, and we are gathered here in a building that is, shall we say, intimidating in its size. But all people everywhere are feeling a bit overwhelmed by bigness, and thoughtful people concerned with how human beings arrange their lives are beginning to see that the very scale of organization is an independent and primary problem. Bigness has a special relationship to pollution. Bigness has a special relationship to genocide, to suicide too; to terrorism and to fatalism—to name but a few ailments highly contemporary. So in such a time it is surely comforting to hear what I take to be the deep-down message of this parable: *small is beautiful. God loves one-talent people.* That's why God made so many of us! And that's why Jesus comes down so hard on this particular one-talent person—because he refuses to believe it. What can you do with someone who refuses to believe it? What can you do with someone who refuses to believe that he or she is loved?

We Americans are today rightly suspicious of those in high office, for the events of recent years have shown us more than we have wanted to know about the arrogance of power. But we tend to forget the degree to which the inertia of the powerless makes possible the powerful. We tend to forget that in God's eyes self-obliteration is just as wicked as self-exaltation. And as this parable makes clear, both stem from the same fateful error of confusing a person's talents with a person's value.

145

Coffin

To one the master gave five, to a second two, and to a third he gave one. To each he gave not according to his value, but "according to his ability." You remember that the two-talent man entered into the same joy of his master as the five-talent man. (That's a lovely phrase, isn't it—"enter into the joy of your master.") What the parable is saying, is that though our talents differ, our value is the same. And the reason for this equality of value, proclaimed on almost every page of the Old and New Testament, is a cornerstone of the Christian faith: God's love does not seek value; it creates it. Our value is a gift, not an achievement. It is not because we have value that we are loved, it is because we are loved that we have value.

I've always loved the story of the beggar in the sixteenth century in Paris, desperately ill, who was brought to an operating table of a group of doctors who said in a Latin they were sure he would not understand, *"Faciamus experimentum in anima vile."* (Let us experiment on this vile fellow.") Whereupon the beggar, actually an impoverished student later to become a world-renowned scholar, Marc Antoine Muret, asked from the slab on which they had laid him out, *"Animan vilem appelas pro qua Christus non dedignatus mori est?"* ("Will you call 'vile' one for whom Christ did not disdain to die?")

What Muret understood so movingly, was that on the cross, God's Son laid bare God's heart for all to see. "This is my body broken for you, this is my blood shed for you—for each and every one of you, because whether you believe it or not, my love for you is greater than any telling of it."

Now why is that so hard to believe? Is it because it's too good to believe—we being strangers to such goodness? But before asking that, let's go on with the parable. After disbursing the talents, the master goes off on a long journey. This too sounds cruel, as if he were some kind of absentee landlord. But here again I think we are dealing with another cornerstone article of the Christian faith: God is a good parent—which is to say, not paternalistic. (*Pater noster non est* paternalistic!) As all of us who strive to be good parents know, love is self-restricting when it comes to power. We cannot exercise our power in such fashion as to restrict the freedom of our children—the freedom to become the independent, mature people God meant them to be. So it is right that the master should have left his servants freedom of choice.

The Spirit and the Power

And now, I think we have arrived at the heart of the parable, the harsh heart, the part that unmasks what we would rather conceal. Most Americans think that the greatness of our democracy is that it offers us freedom of choice. I believe that too. But what that statement overlooks is the present tragedy of American democracy. The present tragedy of American democracy is that although we are offered freedom of choice, most of us, to a startling degree, have lost the ability to choose. I have in mind those who sit in the seats of Congress as well as those who walk the desolate streets of the South Bronx. And I think this is true of our private as well as our public life. The tragedy of our country today is that most of us do not believe that we are loved by God—not really. If we do think so, we don't think so emotionally. Consequently our much vaunted individualism is selfish instead of selfless.

Rather than accepting our value as a gift, we think we have to prove it. We think it derives from the jobs we hold, from the places where we live, from our status and reputation. So unlike the five-talent, unlike the two-talent person, and unlike the blessed saints, whom on this All Saints' Sunday we call to remembrance, we take no chances—not for God's sake. Like the one-talent man, we play it safe, adopting what might be called the protective strategy of deliberate failure. If you don't place any bets you won't lose any money. If you sleep on the floor, you will never fall out of the bed.

Actually, for all his having only one talent, this fellow is shrewd. Deciding that the best defense is offense, he says, "Master, I knew you to be a hard man, reaping where you did not sow, and gathering where you did not winnow." In effect, what he's saying is, "You see, Master, you shouldn't be like that. Look where it gets you. Now of course if you had slipped me five, or even two talents, things might now be different."

Psychiatrists among you might well call this person a passive-aggressive, a passive-aggressive with a punishing instinct. Overcome by fear, he digs, shall we say, his own hole, then tries to punish the master for putting him in it and for not rescuing him from it. When you stop to think of it, it's really surprising that he didn't present the master with a bill for the shovel!

"For God did not give us a spirit of timidity, but a spirit of power and love." What I love about that line is the beautiful implied understanding of our all too human inclination to feel overwhelmed; an understanding that there are always plenty of outer reasons for our inner defeats. At the same time the text ruthlessly insists that what is understandable is also inexcusable. We need not be defeated and we won't be defeated, if instead of colluding with our fears we have the courage of our conviction that God has more love for us than we will ever have hearts ready to receive. That's the choice—every day, almost every hour, and in almost every decision. Will we collude with the fears that tell us, "No, I can't," or with our conviction, hard as it may be to believe, that we are loved with an absolutely overwhelming love. It's a little like this building: either we can feel overwhelmed by its size, or we can allow it to lift up our spirits until we feel with the psalmist, "we are a little lower than the angels."

Finally, it is perfectly true to say that to everyone who has will more be given. For what are we being given? It's not money, it's love. Love begets love; it's power, more power. The greatest reward of love is the opportunity to love more.

So dear friends—old and new—the next time you feel overwhelmed by a sense of your own insignificance, don't reach for the shovel. Remember that God's love doesn't seek value, but creates it. Remember that small is beautiful, that God loves one-talent people. In fact, if our poor wretched earth is ever going to be saved from its present misery, and from the flames that threaten to engulf us, it is going to be rescued by one-talent people like the twelve disciples and all the saints. They became saints very simply because they acted on the belief that there is a divine unquenchable spark in each and every one of us. So, instead of digging, let's start singing: "This little light of mine, I'm going to let it shine—Let it shine, let it shine, let it shine."

November 6, 1977

A Gesture of Reconciliation

On March 5, 1978, Dr. Coffin spoke in Houston, Texas, at the dedica-
tion of a shipload of wheat donated by Midwest farmers and destined
for Vietnam through Church World Service. This communion sermon,
preached the following day at Riverside, focuses on that event and the
need for reconciliation.

YESTERDAY, WITH SEVERAL of you, I was in Houston,
Texas, where the weather was so cold that the distinguished senator
from Iowa, Richard Clark, had to put on his overcoat, something all
politicians have hated to do since the days of John F. Kennedy. But
it was a heartwarming address that he delivered, and everything else
was heartwarming, too, from the dancing of the young women, the
giant puppets led by the Goddess of Wheat, the singing of the gospel
choir, to the mighty praying of the president of the National Council
of Churches, William Thompson. All these took place in a service
dedicated to the sending of ten thousand metric tons of wheat to the
people of Vietnam.

Most moving to me was the moment the farmers and their families came forward to pour a portion of their donated grain into a giant container. Said the five-year-old daughter of one, "I am pouring my grain because all children of the world are friends."

Some Americans, of course, are vigorously opposed to this action. Others are abstaining, fearful to come down on either side of what they conceive to be a hotly debated issue. And most, I fear, are indifferent to this first ship in three years to sail from the shores of the United States to Vietnam. For this indifference, our government is doubtlessly grateful, because since the days of President Ford a total embargo has been imposed on trade and aid, including all food and all medicine. A special permit was difficult to obtain for this particular shipment.

The State Department always likes to take a very complicated view of its own efforts. But the first thing to be said about this shipment of wheat is something very simple. The story of the good Samaritan says that if it is possible to do good without risk or great cost we ought to do good. So, what we celebrated there yesterday, and here today, is no big thing. The shipment of wheat is an act of minimal decency, from a people still committed to a moral world. They are hungry, and we are not; it's as simple as that. And the fact that "they" are Vietnamese has nothing to do with it. If civilians are not a legitimate target in wartime why should they be in peacetime? If, during the war, we tried to spare civilians bombs and bullets, why should we, in peacetime, try to kill them through starvation? It makes neither moral nor logical sense, which is why practically every major power in the world, and endless small countries, are helping reconstruct a country devastated by war and recently pounded by two typhoons. But the one power most present at the destruction is conspicuously absent at the reconstruction. Why?

Had we openly declared war on the Vietnamese, had we fought it as cleanly as possible, had we won it fairly and squarely, I would imagine our government today would be demonstrating a generosity that would make 10,000 tons of wheat look like pittance. Magnanimity is becoming to a victor, generosity is the vanity of giving. Surely those reasons would obtain. But it is also true that our country has a long tradition of generosity going all the way back to words spoken in 1630 by John Winthrop while still on board the *Arabella,* "We must abridge ourselves of our superfluities for the supply of others' necessities." Because we would be at peace with ourselves, we would be making peace with the Vietnamese.

We are still waging war with the Vietnamese today because we are still at war with ourselves. Our nose is out of joint because we didn't win; because our army went to pot—in all senses of that word; because many more soldiers killed many more officers than the army officially recognizes; and because we extricated ourselves from the war as callously as we waged it. But what we should be trying to understand, we are desperately trying to forget. That's why we alone are not at the reconstruction of Vietnam, why we have changed the famous dictum of von Clausewitz around and made politics the extension of war by other means.

Ten thousand metric tons of wheat. For those of you who wonder why it is not rice, let me say that the request came from the Vietnamese themselves. After the long occupation of the French and the more recent American occupation of the south, Vietnamese tastes have changed. They requested wheat milled into bread and noodles. Ten thousand metric tons of wheat will supplement the diet for 200,000 Vietnamese for a year. But just think what 10,000 metric tons of wheat might do for American souls. Were we to search them to seek the errors of our ways, were we to seek peace in our own hearts, we would become peacemakers. The Old Testament prophets preached doom, but only to sinners who denied their sin, to nations whose pride-swollen faces had closed up their eyes. The moment the people heard what the prophets were saying, the moment they saw what the "se-ers" saw—for love is not blind but visionary—at that very moment the prophets began to preach hope, deliverance, peace, reconciliation.

Democracy is a way of distributing responsibility. American Christians have a special responsibility to lead their nation to repentance. What right did we have to decide who lived and died and ruled in Vietnam? To withdraw from one country we had to invade two and bomb three. I myself saw the contents of some of these bombs—twenty thousand little pellets, which could be released silently, eighteen miles away from the victims; and in North Vietnam, I saw what these pellets can do to the entrails of small children. But the war is over. Therefore it is time we ended it in our own hearts, so that we might reach out the hand of friendship to our former enemy. We don't have to approve their form of government. We are not asking our government to send their government arms—that's over. We are only asking that our government send food and medicine. Do you realize that "the starving Indians" have sent 300,000 tons?

A companion, quite literally, is a sharer of the loaf. Soon we ourselves will once again become companions, one of another, by sharing the bread, the body of Christ. But the Vietnamese, too, are our companions, which is why it is quite proper that their pictures should today adorn the church. They are our companions, as ultimately everybody on this planet is a companion. There is only one race—the human race. And the history of that race is a long struggle against all restrictions, a long struggle to affirm that God made us one, that Christ died to keep us that way, so that our sin is only that we are constantly trying to put asunder what God has joined together. For in Christ, "all the fulness of God was pleased to dwell, and through him to reconcile to himself all things, whether on earth or in heaven, making peace by the blood of his cross."

During the war in Vietnam I could not escape the feeling that Christ was between heaven and earth, between the lines, absorbing in his body every pellet and every bullet. And he still is making peace with his blood, until we stop the enmity that divides us, until we fill the hollow in the heart where love should be.

When American troops landed in France during World War I, almost one hundred and fifty years after the American Revolution, General Pershing said, "Lafayette, we are here." Lafayette is remembered far more in this country than he is in France. The same is true of Morrison, the man who outside the Pentagon poured gasoline on himself, lit a match and turned himself into a blazing signpost pointing to the horrors of the war. Here there is no memorial for Morrison. But in Hanoi, a whole broad avenue is named in his honor.

In 1945 as a liaison officer on the frontier between the Russian and the American zones, I watched the Iron Curtain descend. It was cruel. But long after access to the east had been denied all groups, one group could still get through. I had only to say the word "Quakers" and the curtain went up. Every Soviet citizen remembered what the Quakers did to help their starving people in the 1920s. May Church World Service be so remembered in Vietnam.

I am glad we are breaking bread with Christ, with each other, and with the Vietnamese today. For in Christ Jesus, "all the fulness of God was pleased to dwell, and through him to reconcile to himself all things, whether on earth, or in heaven, making peace by the blood of his cross." "This is my body broken for you, this is my blood shed for you." "Come, let us keep the feast."

March 5, 1978

Warring Madness

Dr. Coffin chose the Sunday nearest to the one-hundredth anniversary
of the birth of Harry Emerson Fosdick to call for Riverside to take
leadership in a major new disarmament program. Relating his theme
to Fosdick's sermon, "The Unknown Soldier," and to the then upcom-
ing 1978 United Nations Special Session on Disarmament, Dr. Coffin
urged that we honor Dr. Fosdick by committing ourselves to work
toward a peaceful world.*

IN BROWNING'S *The Ring and the Book,* Pompilia says of her
friend, "Through such souls alone, God stooping shows sufficient of
his light for us in the darkness to rise by."

It is marvelous that in every generation God raises up men and
women with visions larger than their times. These are people who are
for truth, no matter who tells it; for justice, no matter who's against
it. Like God, they carry on a lover's quarrel with the world. It is not
a grudge fight, mind you. If they are against evil it is only because they
so love the good. And if they say the present situation smells to
heaven, it is only because they hold such a bright view of the future.

154

It is not surprising then that we should find that their knowledge still lights our path, their faith lives on in our hearts, and that their tasks have fallen to our hands.

One such person was Harry Emerson Fosdick. To that I can attest because I have read his sermons. But I envy those of you who heard them preached. Sermons are to be heard, rather than read. Preaching is "truth through personality," as Phillips Brooks once described it. I can imagine God's truth through Fosdick's personality Sunday by Sunday, deepening, stretching—sometimes painfully—always enlarging never diminishing the minds and hearts of his hearers. In fact, rereading this week some sermons, it struck me that Fosdick never entertained a diminishing thought or emotion. Oh, I suppose a few came to visit, but I'll bet he never invited them to dinner.

It is wonderful to have so many of you "Fosdick-members" with us today. But I doubt if even the most hoary-headed among you heard the sermon, "Shall the Fundamentalists Win?" This was the one that embroiled him first in public controversy, and it was delivered fifty-six years ago to the day, on May 21, 1922. It was an hour both delicate and dangerous for the church, and Fosdick rose to plead the cause of liberality and tolerance. He said:

I would, if I could reach their ears, say to the fundamentalists about the liberals, what Gamaliel said to the Jews: "Refrain from these men, and let them alone; for if this counsel or this work be of men, it will come to nought; but if it is of God ye cannot overthrow it; lest haply ye be found even to fight against God."

Against the fundamentalists he stated his belief that "finality in the Bible is ahead. We have not reached it. We cannot yet compass all of it." And he ended, where he generally did, at the human crux of the matter:

These last weeks, in the minister's confessional, I have heard stories from the depths of human lives where men and women were wrestling with the elemental problems of misery and sin—stories that put upon a man's heart a burden of vicarious sorrow, even though he does but listen to them. Here was real human need crying out after the living God revealed in Christ. Consider all the multitudes of men [and women] who so need God, and then think of Christian churches making of themselves a cockpit of controversy when there is not a single thing at stake in the controversy on which depends the salvation of human souls.

That is the trouble with this whole business. So much of it does not matter! And there is one thing that does matter—more than anything else in the world—that [people] in their personal lives and in their social relationships should know Jesus Christ.

Fifty-six years later, we still have the intellectual problem of how to incorporate the latest thinking into the old faith, or, as Fosdick put it, "how to believe both in abiding stars and changing astronomies." But more importantly, as then, so even now, we need to seek the grace of magnanimity, the ability to differ and yet love, for if we fail in love we fail in all things else. And it was Fosdick's insight to see the ethical perversion underneath the thological one.

Since coming to Riverside, I have heard many wonderful tales about life in the '30s and '40s, and, in all candor, some not so wonderful. Wealth wielded a lot more influence in those days. Most of the Blacks in the church apparently ran the elevators; yet there were more Blacks in the congregation than women among the trustees, deacons and ushers. And who knows, our membership might still be very much the same had not so many affluent whites in the 1950s been carried off into suburban captivity. (I still think the most enduring feature of the Eisenhower administration will be his federal highway building program.)

But let us not judge the past in terms of the present. In the '30s and '40s there was only one national civil rights organization, and that was founded for the advancement, not the equality of Blacks. And I can remember when I first went to Yale in 1958, thirteen years after Dr. Fosdick had retired, there were, in the entering freshman class at Yale, all of four Black students. As for the women, they received the right to vote only fourteen years before the completion of this building.

Dr. Fosdick would find us poorer in things but richer in soul for the changes that have taken place. He would have been pleased this week to hear Bob Polk, the first Black minister of Riverside, say that he thought that Riverside Church today was probably the most important interracial voluntary association in the city. But let us thank Dr. Fosdick for preparing the way. Time and again he stated that racial discrimination was the most evil thing in the world. It was in response to the depression that he established the arts and crafts program here. And he worried about the church. "I fear," he once said, "for a church like this, where from the pulpit to the pew, we come from privileged backgrounds, when I remember how often in history the underdog has been right."

To honor the memory of so great a person we need some great undertaking. But before describing that undertaking, I want to read to you from another sermon. Bear in mind that only two days from now, the United Nations will convene its first special session on disarmament. This sermon is an Armistice Day sermon, one of the first Dr. Fosdick delivered in this church. It is entitled, "The Unknown Soldier." In it, Dr. Fosdick recalls his own role in World War I, and how war, in fact, does elicit the best in human beings.

They sent men like me into the camps to awaken his idealism, to touch those secret, holy springs within him so that with devotion, fidelity, loyalty, and self-sacrifice he might go out to war. O war, I hate you most of all for this, that you do lay your hands on the noblest elements in human character, with which we might make a heaven on earth, and you use them to make a hell on earth instead. . . . If war were fought simply with evil things, like hate, it would be bad enough, but when one sees the deeds of war done with the loveliest faculties of the human spirit, he looks into the very pit of hell.

He ends up:

O church of Christ, stay out of war! Withdraw from every alliance that maintains or encourages it. It was not a pacifist, it was Field Marshal Earl Haig who said, "It is the business of the churches to make my business impossible." And O my soul, stay out of war!

At any rate, I will do the best I can to settle my account with the Unknown Soldier. I renounce war. I renounce war because of what it does to our own men. I have watched them come in gassed from the front-line trenches. I have seen the long, long hospital trains filled with their mutilated bodies. I have heard the cries of the crazed and the prayers of those who wanted to die and could not, and I remember the maimed and ruined men for whom the war is not yet over. I renounce war because of what it compels us to do to our enemies, bombing their mothers and villages, starving their children by blockades, laughing over our coffee cups about every damnable thing we have been able to do to them. I renounce war for its consequences, for the lies it lives on and propagates, for the undying hatreds it arouses, for the dictatorships it puts in the place of democracies, for the starvation that stalks after it. *I renounce war and never again, directly or indirectly, will I sanction or support another. O Unknown Soldier, in penitent reparation I make you that pledge.*

Dr. Fosdick would be greatly heartened by the UN special session on disarmament—as heartened as he would be disheartened by the fact that neither President Carter nor Mr. Brezhnev plan to attend. He would also be disheartened by the fact that the only proposal the United States ever made since World War II for general disarmament—that was 1962—that proposal is today out of print. And he would be disheartened by the fact that not a single person in the United States government today is charged with the responsibility for thinking about how to end or to reverse the arms race. All they think about in Washingon is arms control, which hasn't worked, and, more importantly, validates the arms that remain.

You don't have to be a pacifist, as was Dr. Fosdick, you can be as anti-Communist as Senator Barry Goldwater; still you can be convinced that each escalation of the arms race provides less and not more security for the peoples of both the United States and the Soviet Union. There is no more military security in military might alone. When national military security has come to depend basically on the reliability with which we do *not* use nuclear weapons, then the "experts" are the experts on human nature.

We are courting disaster. If a nuclear holocaust takes place, not only will millions of innocent civilians here and in the Soviet Union and elsewhere be slain, the ozone layer will be affected, radiation will come through the atmosphere, crops will be poisoned, beasts that remain will eat them, and those who survive the holocaust can be assured of dying of cancer.

And ten years from now we needn't expect terrorists like the Red Brigade to be kidnapping former prime ministers. They will be holding an entire city like New York City hostage with a suitcase bomb.

"Son of Man, I have appointed you as sentry to the House of Israel. When you hear a word from my mouth, warn them in my name." To honor the memory of Dr. Fosdick and the hopes that we all share for the United Nations special session, the deacons of Riverside have unanimously endorsed a national undertaking. For too long, disarmament has been the concern of the antiestablishment. It is time to make it the business of the establishment. To do this, Riverside

Church has employed for one year one of the best organizers in this country, Cora Weiss. She was the one who, for Church World Service, organized the shipment of 10,000 tons of wheat to Vietnam. With the help, I am sure, of many church members, Cora Weiss will organize three convocations under the Riverside roof. To the first, we shall invite all the mayors of the United States and the mayor of Moscow. The subject: Cities or the Arms Race?

To the second we shall invite labor and industrial leaders. The subject: Jobs or the Arms Race? (The arms industry is so capital-intensive that it takes more jobs than it provides. For one billion dollars, you can employ 58,000 people in the arms industry and 145,000 in the job corps, not to mention 73,000 firefighters.)

To the third convocation we shall invite the religious leaders of this nation.

I hope you will all agree that it is right that this church should undertake an educational task of such magnitude. Frankly, I give it about 40 percent chance of success. But let others worry about enterprises that have 80 percent chance of success. We must dream visions larger than our times.

We don't want to cut into the capital of this church: that's other people's money. We want to dig into our own pockets. I am confident that by the end of this week we shall have enough money to launch this program, enough money to ask for matching funds from elsewhere. Already we have received two anonymous gifts of $1,000. All cannot give $1,000, but all can give. And I'll tell you a secret. One of these anonymous donors told me that it was the largest contribution that he was making to charity this year. All of us can match that! In the name of Harry Emerson Fosdick, we can all try to change the arms race into a peace race.

We, too, must carry on a lover's quarrel with the world, so that when, like Harry Emerson Fosdick, we depart this life, we leave behind a little more truth, a little more justice, a little more peace, a little more beauty, than would have been there had we not cared enough about the human race to quarrel with it, not for what it is, but for what it yet might be.

May 21, 1978

Our Resurrection, Too

I AM SURE this freezing morning that none of us needs the reminder found in Haydn's *The Seasons:* "As yet the year is unconfirmed, and oft-returning winter blast the bud and bloom destroy." But never mind, April is on its way. Soon the robins will join the pigeons, the branches will bud, the sky will be filled with the thunder of the sun. Soon overhead, underfoot, and all around we shall see, hear, feel the juice and joy of spring.

But suppose for a moment we knew that April would never arrive. For one terrible moment, pretend that somehow the earth had swung out of orbit and was headed toward the immensities of space, there to be gripped forever in the cold of winter. That, according to Paul, would be a fair presentation of the human world without Easter. For "if Christ has not been raised, your faith is futile and you are still in your sins. Then those also who have fallen asleep in Christ have perished." No doubt about it: Paul puts all his eggs in one Easter basket.

And rightly so. For Christianity is a religion of resurrection, and we shall have to talk about the resurrection event, the empty tomb. But not till later, for it is a common and tragic mistake to view Easter in too narrow, too individualistic a light. Paul makes it abundantly clear that Easter is concerned essentially not with one man's escape from the grave, but with a cosmic victory of seemingly powerless love over loveless power. The lamp of the resurrection doesn't swing over some narrow, empty grave, but rather over the thick darkness covering the whole earth.

On Good Friday the darkness was all but complete, the message clear: fear and hatred kill. And let us not be sentimental, ours is still a Good Friday world. Goodness incarnate stretched out on a cross bequeathing its spirit to the oncoming night is still an apt symbol for a century that has planted more senseless crosses than any other in history, and for a nation which recently planted more than its fair share of such crosses. Today as then we are fearful of living as we are of dying—that is, of thinking boldly, caring deeply, and loving passionately. And when we see someone who is truly alive our instinct is not to emulate that life but to take it away. Never would we have crucified the best among us had we not first crucified the best within us.

But by the light of Easter morn we read through the darkness a "yes, but" kind of message. Yes, hate kills, but love ultimately never dies, never dies with God, never even with us. Love is stronger than death. So the Easter message says essentially that all the tenderness and strength, all the beauty and goodness that on Good Friday we saw scourged, buffeted and stretched out on a cross, all that goodness incarnate is once again alive. "And lo, I am with you always, to the close of the age." Until all eternity Christ will be alive, now in the form of a Holy Spirit trying not only to bring about our resurrection but, through us, to assail and overpower all the demonic forces that corrupt life and bring ruin to the earth. That's why Easter is so decisive an event.

"If Christ has not been raised, your faith is futile." If it's only a Good Friday world, then truth will forever be on the scaffold, wrong forever on the throne. College students, go ahead, take your law boards, play it safe. Christians, retreat from the giant issues of the day into the pygmy world of private piety.

But, says Paul, Christ *has* been raised from the dead. Some of you will say, "well, can you prove it?" To which I am happy to respond, God will never supply evidence to help us make intelligently selfish decisions. In this case it's proof or freedom; the choice for Christ is a free, not a selfish one.

But if the resurrection cannot be proved, it can be known, experienced, and it can be trusted. Faith anyhow is not believing without proof; it's trusting without reservation. The resurrection faith is a willingness—on the basis of all that we have heard, all that we have observed, all that we have thought deeply about, and experienced at a level far deeper than the mind ever comprehends—faith is a willingness to risk our lives on the conviction that while we human beings kill God's love we can never keep it dead and buried. Jesus Christ is risen, today, tomorrow, every day.

There is nothing sentimental about Easter. Resurrection is a demand as well as a promise. Picture, if you will, the disciples shortly after Good Friday. Surely they were grief-stricken. But doubtlessly, too, they were experiencing that sense of relief that comes with resignation from the struggle. "Well, we tried hard, but the Establishment was too powerful. He wasn't elected king. So it's back to fishing, to business as usual." And then comes the word, "He's back."

"Oh no, not again!"

Easter is a demand not for sympathy with the crucified Christ, but a demand for loyalty to the resurrected one. It is a travesty that so often Christians show sympathy for their crucified Christ and at the same time continued loyalty to the institutions that crucified him. Easter, then, is the day to break that loyalty, to say there can be no sympathy without a changed loyalty. The new loyalty must be that of Peter after Jesus' death, the loyalty that made him ten times the person he was before; the same loyalty that made Stephen under the rain of death-dealing stones cry out, Christlike, "Father, forgive"; the loyalty of other martyrs who with their blood watered the seed of the church until it became the acorn that broke the mighty boulder that was the Roman Empire.

There used to be an annual sunrise service on the rim of the Grand Canyon. As the scripture line was read from Matthew, "an angel of the Lord descended from heaven and came and rolled back the stone," a giant boulder was heaved over the rim. As it went crashing down the side of the Canyon, thousands of feet below into the Colorado River, a two-thousand-voice choir burst into the "Hallelujah Chorus." Too dramatic? Not if Paul is correct: we live in an Easter, not a Good Friday world.

But let's move on. The second consequence Paul draws from the resurrection is that we are no longer tied to our sin. I am sure you have all heard of, and many of you have probably read the best-seller *I'm OK, You're OK*. Well, one day there is going to be another best-seller: *I'm Not OK, and You're Not OK and That's OK*. Human beings are never finished products. And we are not perfected because we are not perfectible. Those who think we are, simply show how little they have ever tried to live out their convictions. It's healthy, it's a sign of freedom, to feel guilt about our failures as parents, or as children, or as inhabitants of this city, or as citizens of our nation and world. The only thing that is unhealthy is our failure to believe that there is more mercy in God than sin in us. "Father, forgive them; for they know not what they do." That same forgiveness is alive and well today. So let us not live as sinners, but as forgiven sinners—and what a world of difference there is. Now we can live gratefully, joyfully, not as permanently defeated folk whose contrition has drained all the joy out of their hearts, not to mention the iron out of their spines. So let us give that boulder in the Grand Canyon a second meaning. Let it stand for the burden of guilt which, in Bunyan's *Pilgrim's Progress,* Christian carries on his breaking back up the hill until at last he reaches the cross. There it falls off, and rolls down the hill faster and faster until it disappears into the empty tomb.

And now perhaps we can deal with the empty tomb, the resurrection event. As I am sure many of you know, Paul was the earliest New Testament writer. And it is clear that his resurrection faith, like the faith of the disciples, was not based on the negative argument of an empty tomb, but on the positive conviction that the Lord had appeared to him. It is also clear that Christ's appearances were not those of a resurrected corpse, but much more akin to intense visionary experiences.

The apostles after Jesus' death were ten times the people they were before; that's irrefutable. It was in response to their enthusiasm that the opposition organized; and it was in response to the opposition, many scholars believe, that the doctrine of the empty tomb arose, as a consequence not a cause of the Easter faith. The last chapter of Matthew may be literally true—I don't want to dispute it—but don't let it hang you up indefinitely. The chances are it is an expression of faith rather than a basis of faith.

Convinced by his appearances that Jesus was a living Lord, the disciples had really only one category in which to articulate this conviction, and that is the doctrine of the resurrection of the dead. To Paul, the events of the last days had been anticipated, and God, by a mighty act, had raised Jesus from the dead. To Paul, the living Christ and the Holy Spirit are never differentiated so that when he says, "Not I, but Christ who dwells within me," he is talking about the same Holy Spirit that you and I can experience. I myself believe passionately in the resurrection of Jesus Christ because in my own life I have experienced Christ as a presence, not as a memory. So today on Easter, we gather not to close the show with Bob Hope's "Thanks for the Memory," but rather to re-open the show because "Jesus Christ is risen today. Alleluia."

There remains only to say a word about the third consequence Paul draws from the resurrection. "If Christ has not been raised, then those also who have fallen asleep in Christ have perished. If only in this life have we hope in Christ, we are of all people most to be pitied." What then are we to say of those who now "rest from their labor"? What are we to say as we anticipate our own death?

The Bible is at pains to point out that all life comes to an end. But the Bible also says that not only is God in this world; the world is in God. "He's got the whole world in his hands," which means that our lives run "from God, in God, to God again. Alleluia." Life is eternal, love is immortal, death is only a horizon, and a horizon is nothing save the limit of our sight. We do not know *what* lies beyond, but we do know *who* is beyond the grave. And Christ resurrected links the two worlds, telling us that we really live in only one. Actually, as Paul sees it, if, spiritually speaking, we now die to ourselves and are resurrected in Christ, before us lies only a physical counterpart to this death. And physical death need not be a lifelong terror if fear of the unknown, fear of final condemnation—these fears lie not before us but behind us. Then we can say with that marvelous freedom of Paul, "Whether we live or whether we die, we are the Lord's." "Death, where is thy sting? Grave, where is thy victory? Thanks be to God, who gives us the victory through our Lord Jesus Christ."

He is risen. He is risen, indeed. And so hopefully are we, for did we not sing "Made like him, like him we rise, Ours the cross, the grave, the skies?" So, "Bloom, frozen Christian, April stands before thy door."

March 26, 1978

Whether We Live or Whether We Die

AT THE END of the Easter sermon, I had the distinct and unhappy impression that I had treated death solely as an enemy. To be sure, "Death, where is thy sting; grave, where thy victory?"—these defiant words of Paul imply that death is a threat. But elsewhere Paul speaks differently. Remember what we just heard: "For this slight momentary affliction is preparing for us an eternal weight of glory beyond all comparison." In the first chapter of Philippians he writes, "My desire is to depart and be with Christ, for that is far better." And in the fourteenth chapter of Romans we read "None of us lives to himself, and none of us dies to himself. If we live, we live to the Lord, and if we die, we die to the Lord; so then, whether we live or whether we die, we are the Lord's." These words imply what certainly is true, that death is not the enemy we generally make it out to be.

Often in hospitals, outside the operating room, I have heard surgeons say as they emerge, "We lost her." But did they have her to lose? Back in the '50s Joe McCarthy used to say, "We lost China" as if China had ever been ours to lose. Doctors, be of good cheer. If you don't kill us, you don't fail us. It is enough that you do your best. Our lives are not yours to lose, for "whether we live or whether we die, we are the Lord's."

166

Whether We Live or Whether We Die

Death is far more friend than foe. Suppose we lived forever; we wouldn't live at all. I could imagine my taking two hundred years to decide whether or not to come to Riverside. I can imagine every trustees' meeting lasting at least a month. When you stop to think of it, without death, life would be interminable! Like that little bit of Ireland a Spanish priest once told me about. It reminded him of home, so deaccelerated was the pace. He asked an Irish friend if in Gaelic there was an equivalent for "mañana." Answered the friend: "Oh, yes, we have several expressions like that, but none carry the same sense of urgency as mañana."

I have a private nightmare. We'll live for hundreds of years sitting in armchairs, hooked up to an Empire State Building of extra kidneys and hearts and livers. No, no, it is part of the Good News that life is short. Death brings us to life. So let us address death as would Francis of Assisi: "Brother Death," "Sister Death."

We can say more. As our common destiny, Sister Death enhances our life together. It is often said that death is a great equalizer. But let's be clear: death is an equalizer not because it makes us equal, but because death mocks all our pretensions to be anything else.

In this regard, death is like something else. Werner Pelz writes: *It is a good thing that the king has to take off his crown, that the bishop has to divest himself of his cope and mitre, when they go to bed with their wives. It is a good thing that the great general has to unpin his many decorations, and undo the many layers of glory, even before the slip of a girl that happens to be his mistress. . . . It is a good thing that even the very poor may sometimes take off their shabby clothes to offer themselves to each other in all the richness of any king or queen.*
Before the passion of a man or a woman, as before death, the distinctions of nationality, race, color, ideology become known as the futile and artificial things they finally are.

Death and desire both point to our ultimate human destiny, which is complete and unreserved togetherness. The most beautiful cemeteries in the United States are Indian cemeteries and Moravian cemeteries. I remember years ago in Bethlehem, Pennsylvania, at day's end late in the fall when the leaves were falling, much like in the last act of Cyrano, walking through a Moravian cemetery. I could see all the way across it, because all the tombstones were flat. No pyramids to individual egos there. And when I started to read the

167

names, I found Mr. Schmidt in one row, and Mrs. Schmidt two rows back. When I asked, it was explained, "Oh, yes. When you die you are buried next to the person who died before you." What a way to be buried. What a way to live!

So, thanks be once again to God, who gives us Sister Death to remind us that in life, as in death, we all have more in common than in conflict.

But now let us turn to matters more complicated. Death is also an enemy, but one that can be befriended. In the twelfth chapter of John we find Christ's words, "Truly, truly, I say to you, unless a grain of wheat falls into the earth and dies, it remains alone; but if it dies, it bears much fruit." Christ never urged anyone to die, but rather to live; but to live for something worth dying for, and to die for it if necessary. Certainly that is the complete story of his life, and the most important part of the life of every martyr from Socrates to Martin Luther King Jr.

Try for a moment to imagine how impoverished our lives would be were there no cause worth dying for, or had no one died for such a cause. (Perhaps for the latter to obtain, we would all have to be less sinful, which would be all right.) But the point is this: Until by the grace of God we are sinless, where in the world are we poor sinners going to derive inspiration and strength to contend against our sin, and the sin of the world, if not from the deaths of the likes of Martin Luther King Jr.? What makes this springtime so hard to bear is not the remembrance that ten years ago they shot Martin Luther King and Bobby Kennedy. It's that our lives are not bearing the fruits of their deaths. We are sorry for their deaths, but we are not loyal to their lives. We say we loved them, but we fear to be like them. If we consider the last part of Bobby's life—his days in rural Mississippi, South Africa, his time with Cesar Chavez—we can say of him, as we can of King, "they fought for the poor"; surely a cause worth dying for. But instead of carrying on the struggle, we are seizing their crosses by the other end, turning crosses into swords, and attacking the very people they sought to protect.

Were we loyal to King and Kennedy, not to mention God, the cry today would be "Jobs, not jail." But it's "jail, not jobs." Capital punishment, crime on the streets—once again these are becoming the big electoral issues. Do you realize that we citizens of the richest nation in the world lock up more people per capita than any other industrialized nation in the world, including South Africa? Did you know that the people of Lake Placid could get federal funds for the Olympic Games only by agreeing to allow the Olympic Village that will house the athletes of the world to be turned into a federal prison the moment the athletes depart? From symbol of peace to Gulag! The people of Lake Placid accepted the deal because they were assured five hundred recession-proof jobs. And you can be sure the majority of the inmates will be our people, Blacks and other minorities from New York City. Once again, urban minorities will be guarded by rural whites; another Attica in the making.

The seeds of discord, the roots of crime, lie in the very inequalities we promote in defiance of the great equalizer death. We lock people up largely because we are scared to death of death. That's why we have to befriend the enemy. Of course, we should be scared of crime, but scared to life, to the realization of "jobs, not jails." And until such time as we deal with the true seeds of crime, we must not panic. Whether we live, or whether we die, whether we are mugged or whether we are not mugged, whether we are robbed or not robbed, yes, whether we are raped or whether we are not raped, we are the Lord's. King died that our fear of death would be decreased, not increased.

I hope we can learn, in this violent city, to befriend death. For only when death is befriended does life become human.

I said that death brings us to life, and as our common lot it enhances our life together. Let me finally say a word about how death affects our life with God. It is a strange thing that those closest to God, those who most intensely feel God's presence in every place and moment, these devout people feel the best is still ahead. So Bach writes one of his most beautiful arias, "Come, Sweet Death." And a Black slave writes,

> *I looked over Jordan and what did I see, . . .*
> *A band of angels coming after me,*
> *Coming for to carry me home.*

"My desire is to depart and be with Christ, for that is far better."

I'll tell you what heaven is going to be like. A Dutch theologian once told me. His name is Henri Nouwen. He told me that every time his airplane landed in some airport, he had a fantasy that there would be a voice in the crowd saying "Hey, Henri." There would be somebody who knew him. Each time he would wait for the voice and each time he would be disappointed. But then he would say to himself "It's all right. When I get home my friends will be there." Nevertheless, the fantasy persisted. Every time he landed at a new airport, he would wait for the "Hey, Henri." Each time he'd be disappointed, but then he would remember that when he got home his friends would be there. "So," said Henri, "heaven is going to be like that. God will be there and will say, 'Hey, Henri, how was it? Let's see your slides.' "

"None of us lives to himself, and none of us dies to himself. If we live, we live to the Lord. And if we die, we die to the Lord; so then, whether we live, or whether we die, we are the Lord's." That understanding allows us to befriend death. And fundamentally, we can embrace death as a brother or sister. Then we can be about the all-important task of finding things worth living for that are also worth dying for.

April 9, 1978

Harry Emerson Fosdick, Religious Reformer

by Roger L. Shinn

THE FIRST THING to say is that I'm grateful that, of all the people who would love to do this, I have the privilege of saying something about the public import of Harry Emerson Fosdick.

The next thing is to settle one little rumor. It has been said that Dr. Fosdick taught me to preach. People can't believe it. The evidence is all against it. But the rumor won't quite die. The truth is that I was one of many who took his course in preaching. He listened to our first halting sermons, then criticized them with kindly but penetrating insight. Think of it: America's most influential preacher, listening week after week to the preaching of students, helping us to do better, inviting us to his apartment for tea and sharing the experiences of his ministry. That example was as important as anything he taught.

Through most of his public life Fosdick combined the two vocations of pastor-preacher and seminary teacher. The combination was always fruitful, occasionally amusing. One anecdote, following the publication of Fosdick's book *Adventurous Religion* (1926), has been recorded by both participants. Reinhold Niebuhr, honoring Fosdick's 75th birthday anniversary, wrote it this way in 1953:

When I came to Union a quarter of a century ago I had written an article which was published just after my call to the faculty but before my personal advent at Union. The article, which was written in my brashest and most sophomoric manner, was entitled "How Adventurous Is Dr. Fosdick?" If I remember correctly it chided him for not participating in what was then known as a prophetic criticism of our civilization. I was naturally embarrassed to find myself on the faculty with an eminent man, whom I had treated with little grace. Dr. Fosdick met the situation with characteristic freedom from embarrassment. He invited me to preach for him and after the service bade me to linger in his study.

I'll come back to that record later, but now I'll turn to Fosdick's memory of the same experience in the carbon copy of a letter currently on display in the seminary library. Fosdick says, "From that day on Reinhold Niebuhr and his wife Ursula and the whole Fosdick family have been very cordial friends."

My invitation is to comment on Dr. Fosdick's impact upon that big part of the world that lies outside The Riverside Church. I can best describe him as a religious reformer. I'd like to pronounce that word re-former. The re-former lives in and from a tradition, sometimes re-shaping it, sometimes recovering, sometimes liberating it from stiff encrustations. That is what Fosdick did with Christian tradition.

Let us first look at Fosdick as a reformer of belief and doctrine. Here the central issue was the relating of the Bible to human life in our time. He studied the Bible in Hebrew and Greek. He took it seriously, not as an oracle telling us precisely what to believe and how to behave, but as a scripture to be understood historically.

Thousands of people found help in his book of 1924, coming out of his courses at Union and the Lyman Beecher lectures at Yale, *The Modern Use of the Bible.* For years he taught the course, Practical Theology 27–28, "The Bible in Modern Preaching and Teaching," Tuesday and Thursday at 12 noon. It was elected by about two hundred students, when an entering class at Union was about sixty. The school had to issue tickets to the many students from the university and elsewhere.

Years later he published the longer book, *A Guide to Understanding the Bible.* I heard some of it as lectures on Wednesday nights in the Assembly Hall of Riverside Church. Katharine, not yet my wife, gave it to me for Christmas in 1938.

While a professor at Union, Fosdick became the regular guest preacher at the First Presbyterian Church downtown. When fundamentalists gathered their forces, Fosdick preached his famous sermon of May 21, 1922: "Shall the Fundamentalists Win?"

A furor spread across the country. Long articles appeared on the front pages of newspapers. On Tuesday, January 15, 1923 a seven-column headline in the *New York American* said: "Fosdick 'Whitewashed' in Heresy Investigation." Five hundred members of the New York Presbytery, said the report, listened "with bated breath" in an "atmosphere charged with electricity." The investigating committee criticized the sermon, "Shall the Fundamentalists Win?" It found that its "objectionable" title "tended to contention and strife," and that the sermon was "open to painful misconstruction and just objection." Even so, the committee was trying to be generous. As I read that sermon, what the committee called a "painful misconstruction" was really what Fosdick meant. The committee went on to express confidence in Dr. Fosdick's intention "to promote the gospel and the spread of evangelical truth." That is what the press called a "whitewash."

The quarrel went to the General Assembly of the Presbyterian Church in May 1924. The moderator, Clarence E. Macartney, and the vice-moderator, William Jennings Bryan (then sharpening his oratory for the Scopes trial to come a year later) demanded the ouster of Fosdick. Henry Sloane Coffin of the Madison Avenue Presbyterian Church led forces on the other side.

A compromise prevailed. The General Assembly decided that Fosdick could continue in the pulpit of the First Presbyterian Church *if* he became a Presbyterian. Some of the press described that as a victory for the liberals. *The New York Times* editorial said that it pleased both sides. Fosdick did not see it that way. To become a Presbyterian minister meant subscribing to the Westminister Confession. So he resigned, saying that he was "an evangelical Christian," but that "creedal subscription to ancient confessions of faith is a practice dangerous to the welfare of the church and to the integrity of the individual conscience." *That* for him, he said, would be "moral surrender."

His farewell sermon on March 1, 1925 again filled columns of print on front pages of Monday papers. Soon after came the events that led to the founding of The Riverside Church.

Fosdick, Religious Reformer

The records of those days reveal Fosdick as a self-critical reformer. He was more concerned to affirm Christian faith than to deny specific articles of faith. Rather than glory in his victories, he questioned them. One of his great Riverside sermons was entitled, "The Church Must Go Beyond Modernism." He started by reaffirming the necessity of arriving at modernism. But he criticized its frequent sentimentalism, its tendency to shallowness, its neglect of sin and divine judgment. And he called for a new watchword: "not, Accommodate yourself to the prevailing culture but, Stand out from it and challenge it!"

Second, let us look at Fosdick as a reformer of ministry. Here we can begin by noticing that to many, many people he was above all a guide in personal devotional life. There was that series of books: *The Meaning of Prayer* (1915, then translated into seventeen languages), *The Meaning of Faith* (1917), and *The Meaning of Service* (1920). They were designed for daily reading for the seven days of the week —on each day a passage of scripture, a commentary, and a prayer from the tradition of the church. It was with such books that I learned to pray with Augustine, Anselm, Thomas Aquinas, Martin Luther, Christina Rossetti, Walter Rauschenbusch, and Fosdick.

Another part of Fosdick's ministry was his National Radio Vespers. He became the preacher to thousands of people across the land and eventually, by shortwave, to seventeen countries.

Now and then a story came out of this ministry. For a time Fosdick had a routine, starting with the Sunday sermon at Riverside. On Friday he gave a shortened version of the sermon in the chapel of Union Seminary. Then on the following Sunday afternoon he preached on the radio usually a revised version of the *preceding* Sunday's sermon. One Friday a Union student came to chapel, not yet knowing what he would preach the next Sunday at his Long Island church. He noted the main points and illustrations of Fosdick's sermon, and he used the sermon on Sunday. That night at a church meeting a member told the student: "You know, the funniest thing happened today. I went home from church and heard Fosdick on the radio. And his sermon was so much like yours that, if you hadn't done it first, I would have thought you got it from him!"

Then there was the ministry of counseling. It is characteristic of Fosdick that this master preacher was deeply impressed with the limitations of preaching. It was, he said, as if a person at a third-story window were to let go a drop of medicine with the hope that it would land in the eye of an ailing person in a crowd below. Working with Dr. Thomas W. Salmon and others, he became an innovator in pastoral counseling. Without the experience of personal counseling, he wrote, "I never could have preached for twenty years in Riverside Church." In 1943 he published *On Being a Real Person*. A few months ago John Kauderer found himself sitting on a city bus beside a young man reading the book and entered into conversation with him.

In the threefold contribution of helping people to pray, preaching to a local and international congregation, and exploring new areas of pastoral counseling, Fosdick contributed to the re-formation of pastoral ministry.

Third, Fosdick was a social reformer. From the days of his student ministry on the Bowery, he was concerned about what our society does to people. He held in high admiration Walter Rauschenbusch, the foremost theologian of the Social Gospel.

Among the social issues that concerned him, I suppose the fore most was war. He supported World War I, urging our participation, then preaching to our soldiers in Europe. He was proud when an officer told him he was "worth a battalion." But the cruelty of the war and its outcome convinced him that he could not support another war. He declared himself "ashamed" of his pro-war preaching.

Then came the Nazi menace. *The Christian Century* asked ten influential Christians: "If America is drawn into the war, can you, as a Christian, participate in it or support it?" Fosdick put the answer in one word. "No!" Then he took a few pages to amplify it. He said that he was not neutral between the warring parties in Europe. But he would not endorse war. Even if the United States were invaded, he would support nonviolent resistance—though he knew this country was not ready for so demanding a policy.

I agreed when he said, "I will not use my Christian ministry to bless war." But then I dissented. I saw the war as a tragic necessity, and I went off to fight. When I returned, I came promptly to Riverside to worship, still wearing a combat officer's uniform because I owned no other clothes. At the close of the service I approached the chancel to greet Dr. Fosdick and introduce my wife, whom he had never met.

And I realized that he had kept his pledge, in that same article in *The Christian Century,* to "minister alike to the needs of the conscientious objector and the conscientious soldier."

In his hymn that we love to sing we ask the "God of grace and God of glory" to "cure thy children's warring madness." It was a sound instinct that led Bill Coffin on the Centennial Sunday, to call his sermon "Warring Madness."

I should mention also Fosdick's interest in this neighborhood. He and Father George Ford of Corpus Christi Church and Rabbi Louis Finkelstein of the Jewish Theological Seminary worked together in mutual trust. Dr. Fosdick was president—I think the first president —of the Manhattanville Community Centers.

Now I want to go back to that story of Fosdick and Niebuhr, and read the rest of Niebuhr's account of the meeting in the study:

He told me, without referring directly to any attack upon him, that it was his conviction that each generation had only one battle in its system and would have to trust the next generation to fight subsequent battles. There was a special quality in this modest disclaimer; for Dr. Fosdick proved in two decades of preaching at the new Riverside Church that no one in our generation could illumine the ethical issues which modern man faced in our technical society with greater rigor and honest discrimination than he.

We have looked at a religious reformer in three dimensions of his life: the doctrinal, the pastoral, and the social. One sign of his leadership is that as we look back to him, we find him bidding us look forward. He had an uncanny ability to sense the needs of his time, then not to echo but to meet them.

When challenged by the fundamentalists as to the finality of the Bible, he answered: "Finality in the Bible is ahead. . . . God is leading us toward it." When he said, "The Church Must Go Beyond Modernism," he ended that sermon with these words: "We cannot harmonize Christ himself with modern culture. What Christ does to modern culture is to challenge it."

Harry Emerson Fosdick puts to us that challenge today.

May 24, 1978